# AROUND los angeles WITH KIDS

### by Lisa Oppenheimer

Fodor's Travel Publications
New York • Toronto • London • Sydney • Auckland

www.fodors.com

## CREDITS

**Writer:** Lisa Oppenheimer

**Series Editors:** Karen Cure, Caroline Haberfeld
**Editor:** Andrea Lehman
**Editorial Production:** Tom Holton
**Production/Manufacturing:** Robert Shields

**Design:** Fabrizio La Rocca, *creative director*;
Tigist Getachew, *art director*
**Illustration and Series Design:** Rico Lins, Keren Ora
Admoni/Rico Lins Studio

## ABOUT THE WRITER

Lisa Oppenheimer, mother of two, is a contributor to *Disney, Sesame Street Parents,* and *Car Travel* magazines.

### Fodor's Around Los Angeles with Kids

First Edition
ISBN 0–679–00489–0
ISSN 1526–1387

**Important Tip**

Although all prices, opening times, and other details in this book are based on information supplied to us at press time, changes occur all the time in the travel world, and Fodor's cannot accept responsibility for facts that become outdated or for inadvertent errors or omissions. So always confirm information when it matters, especially if you're making a detour to visit a specific place.

**Special Sales**

Fodor's Travel Publications are available at special discounts for bulk purchases for sales promotions or premiums. Special editions, including personalized covers, excerpts of existing guides, and corporate imprints, can be created in large quantities for special needs. For more information, contact your local bookseller or Special Markets, Fodor's Travel Publications, 201 East 50th Street, New York, NY 10022. Inquiries from Canada should be directed to your local Canadian bookseller or sent to Random House of Canada, Ltd., Marketing Dept., 2775 Matheson Boulevard East, Mississauga, Ontario L4W 4P7. Inquiries from the United Kingdom should be sent to Fodor's Travel Publications, 20 Vauxhall Bridge Road, London, England SW1V 2SA.

PRINTED IN THE UNITED STATES OF AMERICA
10 9 8 7 6 5 4 3 2 1

# CONTENTS

# WELCOME TO GREAT DAYS!

**B**etween pick-ups, drop-offs, and after-school activities, organizing a family's schedule is one full-time job. Planning for some fun time together shouldn't be another. That's where this book helps out. In creating it, our parent-experts have done all the legwork, so you don't have to. Open to any page and you'll find a great day together already planned out. You can read about the main event, check our age-appropriateness ratings to make sure it's right for your family, pick up some smart tips, and find out where to grab a bite nearby.

## HOW TO SAVE MONEY
Taking a whole family on an outing can be pricey, but there are ways to save.

**1.** Always ask about discounts at ticket booths. We list admission prices only for adults and kids, but an affiliation (and your ID) may get you a break. If you want to support a specific institution, consider buying a family membership up front. Usually these pay for themselves after a couple of visits, and sometimes they come with other good perks—gift-shop and parking discounts, and so on.

**2.** Keep an eye peeled for coupons. They'll save you $2 or $3 a head and you can find them everywhere from the supermarket to your pediatrician's office. Combination tickets, sometimes offered by groups of attractions, cost less than if you pay each admission individually.

**3.** Try to go on free days. Some attractions let you in at no charge one day a month or one day a week after a certain time.

## GOOD TIMING

Most attractions with kid appeal are busy when school is out. Field-trip destinations are sometimes swamped on school days, but these groups tend to leave by early afternoon, so weekdays after 2 during the school year can be an excellent time to visit museums, zoos, and aquariums. Outdoors, consider going after a rain—there's nothing like a downpour to clear away crowds. If you go on a holiday, call ahead—we list only the usual operating hours.

## SAFETY CATCH

Take a few sensible precautions. Show your kids how to recognize staff or security people when you arrive. And designate a meeting time and place—some visible landmark—in case you become separated. It goes without saying that you should keep a close eye on your children at all times, especially if they are small.

## FINAL THOUGHTS

We'd love to hear yours: What did you and your kids think about the places we recommend? Have you found other places we should include? Send us your ideas via e-mail (c/o editors@fodors.com, specifying the name of this book on the subject line) or snail mail (c/o Around Los Angeles with Kids, Fodor's Travel Publications, 201 East 50th Street, New York, NY 10022). In the meantime, have a great day around Los Angeles with your kids!

### THE EDITORS

# ADVENTURE CITY

I f your children jump for joy when the carnival trailers unfurl their awnings, they'll be in heaven in Adventure City. A mini amusement park designed just for younger kids, Adventure City is an upscale version of the familiar fairs on wheels you see setting up shop in the summer, with scaled-down rides kids enjoy and scaled-down prices (relative to the theme-park giants) that parents appreciate. In fact, if you spend most of your time at the kiddie section of the bigger theme parks, you're much better off here.

The entire park is set up like a tiny town; there's a police station, train depot, and airport. Many of the 17 rides and attractions are of the spin-till-you're-queasy variety that kids love. Fortunately, since you may be accompanying your children on some attractions, there are a number of non-stomach-churning rides to choose from, including a pint-size roller coaster and Ferris wheel, as well as a "crazy" school bus and a vintage miniature train driven by an affable engineer. One of the cutest of the lot is the Crank and Roll ride, where kids use their own steam to power a miniature train along a track. The park's first full-size roller coaster,

**HEY, KIDS!** There are a few things you should definitely not forget to do. Don't miss the tour of the police/fire station, where you can drive your own Adventure City emergency vehicle. And before you leave, remember to trade in your arcade winnings. Once outside the park, visit the mass of collectibles that is Hobby City, the original "City" that spawned the amusement park. If you're a doll fan, check out the Anaheim Doll & Toy Museum, in the White House, an impressive half-scale replica of that famous Washington home.

10120 Beach Blvd., between Ball Rd. and Cerritos Ave., Stanton

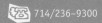
714/236-9300

$11.95 ages over 1 yr

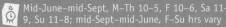
Mid-June–mid-Sept, M–Th 10–5, F 10–6, Sa 11–9, Su 11–8; mid-Sept–mid-June, F–Su hrs vary

10 and under

the new Tree Top Racer, will placate older siblings, but it may be too wild for wee ones—even those who make the 42" height requirement. Other than rides, kids can choose from several fun activities. Animal lovers can visit with llamas, sheep, goats, rabbits, and chickens, among others, at the petting farm, while train enthusiasts can create their own track configurations at the vast Thomas the Tank Engine and Friends play area. There are live, interactive performances—puppet shows, sing-alongs, story times, and the like—held regularly at the outdoor theater, and your children can leave with painted faces and armloads of prizes from the park's arcade games.

Adventure City is also the perfect party place, with special packages available to celebrate your child's birthday. But then every day's a party at this festive amusement park.

**KID-FRIENDLY EATS** Adventure City has snack carts spread around, but the only place to get hot food is at **Parker's.** Outside the park, try the **Restaurant Next to the White House** (Hobby City, 1238 S. Beach Blvd., Anaheim, tel. 714/827–0584), a little homespun place that serves comfort food for breakfast and lunch and has an apt name, to boot.

**KEEP IN MIND** Even though this isn't a mega-amusement park, plan on a trip here being a full-day event. Making that easier is Adventure City's pay-one-price admission, enabling your children to ride their favorites endlessly without repeatedly dipping into your pockets. Of course, any money you feel like you've saved can easily be dropped on arcade games and souvenir shops spread around the park.

# ADVENTURE PLAYGROUND

This is the place to get down and dirty. A small slice of kid heaven in the middle of larger Huntington Central Park, Adventure Playground nevertheless packs much into its roughly ¾-acre confines, with mud, slides, tire swings, and a lot of appealing rough-and-tumble activity.

Your children will first encounter a small, manmade pond, where budding Huck Finns use mini-rafts and stick poles to get from one side to the other. Alongside, kids fly along on a tire attached to an overhead zip-line. Behind the pond sits the beloved mud slide and its grand finale: a splash landing in a delightfully muddy puddle.

But the most original part of the park—certainly the most memorable—is in back. At what amounts to a life-size erector set, your children can saw, hammer, and nail away, building actual structures they can then play inside. Staff members provide the building materials (two-by-fours, slabs of plywood, and even old tires) and tools (small hammers, dull saws); kids provide the imagination. Some add on to preconstructed tree houses; others start

## HEY, KIDS!
The mud slide is open sporadically during the day so make sure to be around for at least a few runs. When it's closed, head to the construction area. Though you can add to an existing structure, don't be shy about starting something new. At the end you'll be able to say, "I built it myself!"

**KEEP IN MIND** Adventure Playground's downscale charm can keep kids occupied for a whole day. Surprisingly, however, weekdays tend to be the most crowded, because the park is popular among camp groups; to avoid the rush, visit on a Saturday. Your children should wear sneakers that you don't mind getting trashed, as they are required in all park areas, including the water (no sandals allowed). Outdoor showers are available for post-mud rinsing. Children under 5 are admitted but cannot swim without a parent in the water. Reservations are recommended for groups of 10 or more.

from scratch. The result is an amalgam of creative play spaces from wooden mazes to tepees to race cars. Sound structures are left standing until the park closes for the season at summer's end. Budding architects have been known to spend an entire day in the construction site. Adventure Playground has a small but extremely congenial staff of teens (plus an adult administrator) to lend a hand, but parents are expected to be the primary supervisors.

According to park operators, you needn't be skittish about either the neighboring Chevron holding station—admittedly an eyesore—or the park "dirt." Though the water looks murky, it's actually quite clean thanks to a cement bottom and regular water changing. And as for your children and their clothes, well, it should all come out in the wash.

*KID-FRIENDLY EATS* Located inside Huntington Central Park, the **Park Bench** (17732 Golden West St., tel. 714/842–0775) serves breakfast and lunch daily. **Norm's** (16572 Beach Blvd., tel. 714/841–1919) serves a typically enormous 24-hour chain-restaurant menu.

# ANGELS ATTIC

It's called a "museum" of toys, but the austere title doesn't seem to do it justice. A lovingly collected assortment of turn-of-the-century dollhouses, miniatures, and other classic playthings, Angels Attic is more like a warm, fuzzy "attic" full of treasures that will likely make everyone—kids and adults alike—feel like they've happened upon a visit to grandma's.

On two floors of a restored 1895 Victorian house, Angels Attic emits that homey feeling from the moment you step through the wicker-furnished front porch. Once inside, it's hard not to be struck by the awesome spread of dollhouses on the home's first floor—big, small, elaborate, simple—you name it. Some are antiques; others have been commissioned for the Attic. Among the favorites are a boot-shape structure reminiscent of the "Old Woman Who Lived in a Shoe" rhyme; Tara, complete with Rhett and Scarlett; and a Lilliputian Versailles. Many kids scoot around the room simply agog at the display, while others peer wide-eyed into tiny windows, exclaiming things like "Mommy, you'll never believe what's in here!" The interiors are indeed as amazing as the exteriors. Inside are curved stairways and elaborate scenes of Victorian tranquillity, from a mother-child story time by a fireplace to perfectly arranged place settings on tiny dining room tables.

**HEY, KIDS!** There are all sorts of treasures waiting to be discovered here. When taking in the shoe-shape house, look for the toy shop (complete with proprietor) set into the heel. Also, see how many of the dozens of pairs of animals you can name in the Noah's Ark display, and ask one of the hostesses to turn on the antique toy train.

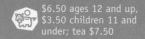

Upstairs is reserved for a collection of elaborate dolls, porcelain and otherwise. Among the highlights here are the dolls on the stair landing, posed, dressed up, and decorated to celebrate each season.

Though by necessity a "do not touch" institution (you wouldn't, after all, want to be responsible for breaking any of these treasures), Angels Attic is nonetheless unusually child friendly. You'll certainly be expected to keep an eye on your children, but staff here—mostly volunteers as this is a nonprofit, charitable institution—seem tirelessly patient and fond of the little ones, adding yet another element to that grandma's-house feel. You can add still more to the old-time experience by reserving a teatime (tea, lemonade, and light pastries served) out on the house's sunny front porch.

**KID-FRIENDLY EATS** **Tudor House** (1403 2nd St., tel. 310/451–4107) serves English foods in a traditional English Tea Room. Across the street, **Fritto Misto** (601 Colorado Ave., tel. 310/458–2829) serves various Italian favorites, like pastas.

**KEEP IN MIND** While there are some items for sale here (count on at least a few squeals of "I want that!"), most are quite pricey. Still, there is a basket full of less expensive collectibles that kids can rifle through, as well as a comfortable book corner for buying or browsing, not to mention spending a quiet moment with a story. And when you're done here, you can head to the Santa Monica Pier, just five blocks away, for a fitting end to your day.

# AQUARIUM OF THE PACIFIC IN LONG BEACH

This relatively new aquarium is one of those places that amply succeeds in its dual role as entertainer and educator. You get to spend a great day marveling at some amazing animals, and you can count on walking away feeling that you and your children have actually learned something. In fact, your kids are sure to like this place, a splashy and colorful spot that brings sea creatures—everything from playful puffins and Japanese spider crabs to rock fish and a 6-foot sea bass—as close as possible without your having to don wet suits.

Divided into three areas, the aquarium focuses on three major ocean regions: Tropical Pacific, Northern Pacific, and California Baja. Designers have amply succeeded in getting you nose-to-gill with the scaly inhabitants (more than 10,000 animals in all), particularly in the Plexiglas tunnel aquariums, where water and fish surround you on all sides but beneath. The effect is particularly enthralling in the Coral Tunnel in the Tropical Pacific, where colorful tropical fish seem to envelop you. (The exhibit is actually designed after a popular tropical reef off the island of Palau, in Micronesia.) The scuba feeling is enhanced further by the

**KID-FRIENDLY EATS** The aquarium's **Café Scuba** offers a food court–style selection of burgers, sandwiches, and snacks. Or grab the free shuttle to one of the downtown Long Beach eateries, including **Johnny Rockets** (245 Pine Ave., tel. 562/983–1332), a '50s–retro burger joint.

**KEEP IN MIND** Since its opening in 1998, the aquarium has proved extremely popular, scaring away some would-be visitors who feared it would be too crowded. Year-two attendance, however, has settled down to more manageable levels. Even so, try off-peak hours, roughly weekdays after 1 or weekends by 9 or 10. Both times should get you in the door line-free.

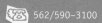

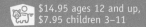

appearance of real divers, who submerge regularly to feed the fish. Another popular spot is the outdoor seating area, where you can take a gander at perennial kids' favorites, such as harbor seals and sea lions.

For those who'd like to do more than just look, there are Discovery Labs for feeling the likes of sea urchins, crabs, and the snail-like sea hare. At the ever-popular skate and ray touch pools, your curious youngsters can reach out and touch the slippery stingray (stingers removed) and its relatives. Small children can scurry about at the Kid's Cove, pretending to be hermit crabs in the sand or walking through the "bones" of a giant gray whale skeleton. Now, you can't do that just anywhere!

**HEY, KIDS!** While in the California Baja tunnels, see if you can get a sea lion to follow your finger. When they're in the right mood, the lively animals love to play along. But first, you'll have to get their attention, either with large movements or by waving a bright hat. In the Tropical Pacific area, look for leafy sea dragons. Related to sea horses, they're often hard to spot because they resemble weeds. Can you think why that would come in handy?

# ATLANTIS PLAY CENTER

If you're tired of the theme-park bustle (not to mention overstimulated kids!), you'll find a welcome respite in this pleasing theme playground. Located in the larger Garden Grove Park, this much-loved playground is remarkable for its very ordinariness: one of those places you plan to go for an hour and wind up spending the entire day.

As the name suggests, the creative park is based on the famed lost city, although the ocean under which it's submerged must be invisible, as there is no water here save for a fountain or two. Spread inside a wooded 4-acre park are roughly 15 play sites, including sand-digging areas where climb-on sea creatures poke their heads out of the sand. Your children can zip down a whale slide and pop out through the orca's mouth or engage in all sorts of seafaring play around a beached Viking ship. The most beloved fixture here, by far, is the enormous Dragon Slide. Apart from kids' affinity for it, the slide rekindles a bit of nostalgia in parents, who can often be heard reminiscing about their own endless childhood slides down the thing. (The park has been a fixture since the 1960s.)

KEEP IN MIND  Sometimes, this play center can be the ideal, quiet setting; at others, the quiet is drowned out by noise. One source is a highway in close proximity to one of the park's boundaries, so be prepared for some traffic sounds. Another is the kids themselves. The park can get crowded with a capital "C," especially on Wednesdays and Thursdays, when the park often entertains school groups. And although the literature states "for ages 3–12," many parents feel it's more suited for those up to only 9 or 10.

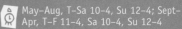

Though the equipment here makes this like other slightly revved-up playgrounds, what sets it apart is its setting. Atlantis is completely enclosed, with only one (attended) door through which you enter or exit. The added security allows you the luxury of enjoying a shady spot while giving your kids more freedom to play. Though you are still responsible for your children at all times, there are staff people on hand to keep the place in order. That means, among other things, that you'll get official reinforcement when you tell your youngster not to climb *up* the slide. And the fact that you have to pay to get in means that there's always somebody at the gate keeping adults from entering without a child and children from leaving without a parent.

*KID-FRIENDLY EATS* Atlantis has lots of greats picnic spots. If you forget to bring your own, have your hand stamped at the gate; you can then pick up eats at one of the numerous fast-food joints on Brookhurst Street and return. A **snack bar** operates in the park daily in summer and weekends the rest of the year. If you'd prefer something a little warmer, try **SouPlantation** (5939 W. Chapman Ave., tel. 714/895–1314), which serves a buffet of soup, salad, and pastas.

# AUTRY MUSEUM OF WESTERN HERITAGE

The cowboy music playing in the plaza as you enter the museum is a tip-off to what's inside. Decades after Hollywood immortalized the American west via the Lone Ranger and Little Joe Cartwright, the Autry came along (in 1988) to give a real-life but fun look at this romanticized segment of American culture.

Your little cowpokes will probably want to head straight to the museum's Children's Discovery Gallery—a real gem. Within it, a cottage—a small-scale replica of an actual Arizona ranch house—comes complete with vintage family photos and actual cowboy duds like chaps, hats, and boots that they can hustle into before climbing into the saddle on a full-size fiberglass horse. Upstairs there are more period clothes to try on as well as some old-fashioned wooden games to play. The pre-electric kitchen comes stocked with "food" for cooking on the range and a washboard that illustrates the challenge of doing laundry pre-Maytag.

## HEY, KIDS!

Climb on the saddle in the upstairs Spirit of Imagination gallery. The "horse" sits in front of a "blue screen," and through the magic of special effects, you can see yourself galloping along on the range.

**KEEP IN MIND** Though the facility bears the name of benefactor Gene Autry, don't expect a lot of exhibits dedicated to the famed movie cowboy. Mr. Autry, who died in 1998, mandated that the museum be used for American history, as opposed to Gene Autry history—hence the appearance of but one small showcase about the man himself. Before you come, ask about the museum's educational programs. The unusually creative and interesting special events include family festivals, ethnic arts and crafts, and storytelling. On some weekends, you can have souvenir photos taken in period garb.

 4700 Western Heritage Way, I–5 and Rte. 134

 323/667–2000

 $7.50 adults, $5 youths 13–17, $3 children 2–12

 T–Su 10–5

 3 and up

Paraphernalia in other parts of the museum is equally sure to please. Life-size dioramas of the Old West include a full-size stagecoach, a saloon, and re-created scenes, such as the Earps and Clantons at the OK Corral. Kids can "lock up" their siblings in the authentically re-created jail (don't worry; the structure has only three sides) or ponder the weight of the cumbersome clothing ladies wore ("glittering misery," as these dresses were called). Upstairs you'll find a collection of western art as well as a tribute to western movie-making that contains a mosey-through street scene, famous film and television artifacts (look for the Lone Ranger's mask), and videos about western stunts. Despite its relatively small size, the outdoor Trails West exhibit does a nice job depicting the region's natural terrain, including rock formations, a pond, and a waterfall.

**KID-FRIENDLY EATS** The on-site **Golden Spur Cafe** is known for its shoot-'em-up homemade chili but serves burgers, hot dogs, sandwiches, and salads as well. The **Crocodile Café** (626 N. Central Ave., Glendale, tel. 818/241–1114) serves pastas, salads, sandwiches, and pizzas as well as a separate children's menu.

# CABRILLO MARINE AQUARIUM

This aquarium on the beach is more of a marine education center than a simple tourist attraction, and that is precisely the fun of this intimate facility on the San Pedro coast. It's a place where families can not only look at tanks full of marine life, but also go out in the wild with the experts and explore.

A visit to the museum can be split into two parts. Inside, roughly 7,500 square feet of exhibit space contains 35 aquariums displaying southern California marine life. Some of the habitats include touch tanks, and many feature hands-on activities. The facility also houses a small research laboratory that doubles as an aquatic nursery, where such creatures as jelly fish are raised. The lab is open to the public; in fact, visitors are often invited to become involved in research projects (as researchers, not subjects!).

Though the interior tanks are indeed beautiful, outside is where the aquarium's individuality really shines. With harbor and ocean beaches right at its front door, the facility is equipped

**KEEP IN MIND** The aquarium runs several special programs that might interest your family, so it's a good idea to call before you come in order to find out what's happening when. Grunion programs occur twice monthly from March to July, but since they don't begin until 9 PM, they are better for older children. Tide-pool tours are given on most weekends, and though reservations are not required, you'll still want to call ahead to check on the schedule, which is dependent on low tide. During the winter, the aquarium runs two-hour whale-watching tours to see the migration of the California gray whales.

for such natural explorations as tide pooling, which takes place most weekends. One of the most popular events is the annual grunion program. During spawning season (March to July), the small, native southern California grunion swims in to deposit its eggs in the sand; if you visit on a selected night during this time, you can join a staff-led foray to watch the spectacle of literally thousands of these silver fish surfing up to the shore. Normally, the eggs remain buried and unhatched until the tide washes them free. Occasionally, however, Cabrillo staff retrieve eggs that can be hatched in the lab by visitors who add sea water and a good shake.

You can also participate in one of the aquarium's nature workshops. Wednesday afternoons, look for free Marine Lab programs with games, crafts, and other activities aimed at aquatic education.

**TRANSPORTATION** Getting to the aquarium, decidedly off the beaten path, can be a little tricky if you don't know where you're going. Take I–110 to the Harbor Boulevard exit; turn right on Harbor Boulevard and right again on 22nd Street. Then turn left on Pacific Avenue, and take it to Stephen White Drive.

**KID-FRIENDLY EATS** The **Lighthouse Deli** (508 W. 39th St., tel. 310/548–3354) serves breakfast and lunch deli favorites. The friendly **Pacific Diner** (3821 S. Pacific Ave., tel. 310/831–5334) is presided over by owner Dennis Jewett and family, who serve up comfort-food favorites (meat loaf, pot roast) as well as some Mexican-inspired egg dishes for breakfast and lunch daily.

# CALIFORNIAN

If you've ever wondered about the on-board life of a nineteenth-century sailor, wonder no more. The tall ship *Californian* is the place to find out. A replica of an 1848 revenue cutter (some may actually recognize it from the Steven Spielberg film, *Amistad*), the *Californian* takes on guests to experience what life was like at sea a century and a half ago.

During the four-hour sails, which travel roughly 5 miles along the California coast, everybody becomes a crew member for a day. Jobs include hauling lines for raising the sails, weighing the anchor (raising it, not finding out how heavy it is), and even taking a turn at the helm to steer the gallant vessel. Don't worry: Real crew members assume the dicey task of climbing those 100-foot masts to unfurl the sails, and no one is ordered to swab the deck. There's also a cannon demonstration, although you'll have to rely on the professionals to do the firing.

In addition to manual tasks, a trip on the *Californian* yields some practical lessons in the math and science (oceanography) behind navigation and boat speed. You'll learn

## HEY, KIDS!

Be prepared to use some muscle to raise those sails. They may look airy, but these behemoths—made of canvas instead of the lighter, synthetic materials used today—can stretch 60 feet and weigh 800 pounds. To get them up, you'll need strength—yours and your crewmates'.

## KEEP IN MIND

The *Californian* sails from several cities on the California coast, so you'll have to call to find out when it's expected in port here. Though the passenger requirement is listed as 40 pounds and up (roughly 6 years old), for safety reasons, it's recommended that you wait until children are at least 9. Remember that this is a fully interactive trip, and falling asleep on the job is a definite no-no. If you opt for a seasickness remedy, make sure it's a non-drowsy formula, and take it one hour ahead.

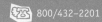

firsthand the value of teamwork, perhaps the most significant element in maneuvering the ship.

Voyage hosts weave in tales of life aboard the original ship, the *Lawrence,* a craft that operated as an 1840s version of a coast-guard vessel. That and the fact that the ship has been so painstakingly re-created—except for the addition of modern-day safety equipment—help you experience living history.

Though everyone, including kids, is expected to do their part—half the fun, after all—this is not all work and no play. "Crew members" on the *Californian* have plenty of time to enjoy the scenery, not to mention the hearty seafarer's lunch served on board. Devout landlubbers don't have to miss out completely; the Nautical Heritage Society, the group that owns the ship, occasionally opens it for tours while it's moored at the dock (no charge).

### KID–FRIENDLY EATS

**Stefano's** (429 Shoreline Dr., tel. 562/437–2880) offers some ultratasty pizza in Long Beach's nearby Shoreline Village. **Papa's Western BBQ and Saloon** (5305 Pacific Coast Hwy., tel. 562/597–4212) is exactly what it sounds like, with an open-pit barbecue and lots of finger-licking entrées. Also *see* restaurants in the Aquarium of the Pacific in Long Beach, *Queen Mary,* and *Scorpion.*

# CALIFORNIA SCIENCE CENTER

The California Science Center is one of those facilities that seems to be routinely showing up on kids' "favorite" lists these days. Opened in 1998, this nifty place is no "look but don't touch" showroom, but rather a tinkerer's paradise where gizmos and gadgets bring to life many of those science principles your young students have been learning about in the classroom.

Most of the center's permanent exhibits are divided between two galleries: the World of Life and the Creative World. World of Life is where you can get a leg up on the living body—human, animal, or plant—through any number of activities. Your children can take a virtual tour through the human circulatory system via a red blood cell or watch the body's physiological changes via a multimedia presentation of Tess, the translucent 50-foot woman.

The Creative World explores technology, and this is where your curious ones will find the real toys: digital wizardry that allows them to "morph" their own photographed image, a

**KEEP IN MIND** All the neat toys here can make hours go by in what seems like moments, so plan to stay at least half a day. Head to the high-wire bicycle early, as the attraction usually has a line later on. For further explorations, ask about the institution's Science Workshops (extra charge), for kids pre-K to 10th grade. These weekend classes, held in rooms just outside the main facility, use science center–style approaches to learning such sciences as chemistry, physics, and biology.

700 State Dr.

 323/724-3623

 Free; IMAX $7.50 adults, $6 students 13–17, $4.75 children 4–12; high-wire bicycle $3.50

 Daily 10–5

 5 and up

computerized musical jam session, and a video periscope that lets them chat with tourists in other areas of the building. And that's just the beginning. Each gallery also has a discovery room, where younger kids can conduct hands-on activities with Mom and Dad or see live animals, such as butterflies, frogs, mice, and snakes. The center also has a special-exhibits gallery, containing an ever-changing series of traveling exhibits.

Of course, a visit to the center wouldn't be complete without a ride on the high-wire bicycle, a display about the force of gravity masquerading as a circus act. Strung across a wire three stories up, the bicycle seems to defy gravity, allowing strapped-in riders to pedal back and forth without tipping over. (The feat is accomplished thanks to a weight on the bicycle's underside.) And don't miss the much-raved-about IMAX theater, where 3-D features are shown on a giant, seven-story screen.

**HEY, KIDS!** Try out your architectural prowess by constructing your own earthquake-proof building (materials provided). Your structure is a success if it stays up once the simulated earthquake mechanism starts moving and shaking. But don't despair if yours doesn't make it. To date, very few structures have passed the test.

**KID-FRIENDLY EATS** The science center has a choice of three convenient places to eat: **Megabites Cafe,** which has pizza, salads, and a grill; the self-explanatory **McDonald's;** and the quiet **Rose Garden Cafe,** which serves coffee, dessert, and sandwiches (but usually not in that order) overlooking the historic rose garden. You can also sample the Korean-influenced fare at **Woo Lae Oak** (*see* the Los Angeles County Museum of Art).

# CAROLE & BARRY KAYE MUSEUM
## OF MINIATURES

There's something about things unusually large or unusually small that seems to capture kids' imaginations. The latter is what you'll find at the Carole & Barry Kaye Museum of Miniatures, a quasi-big museum of little things.

Here you'll find incredibly elaborate structures that *could* fit snugly into the palm of a child's hand—that is, if children were allowed to touch the exhibits, which they're not. But your children can feel a little like Alice looking at a shrunken Wonderland, peering into pint-size replicas of some unlikely structures, such as the Vatican, the Opera House at Versailles, and the Hollywood Bowl, complete with musicians, instruments, and vocal legends. Though the significance of the structures will probably be lost on little ones, they can still engage in the fantasy of imagining themselves small enough to live inside, while you are busy marveling at the perfect detail in such diminutive forms.

**KEEP IN MIND** Though the subject matter here will certainly interest young children, bringing them here is not the most effortless experience. The staff here are cordial enough, if not exactly warm and fuzzy. They absolutely expect you to keep an extra-close watch on your children and forbid kids to enter the gift shop unsupervised. And in addition to the "look but don't touch" aspect, which can be hard for the littlest and most curious viewers to understand, the museum's tall displays require you to repeatedly lift wee ones up to see, which can be hard for you if you have a tired or weak back.

5900 Wilshire Blvd.

 323/937-6464

 $7.50 adults, $5 students 12–21, $3 children 5–11

T-Sa 10-5, Su 11-5

4 and up

Open since 1993, the museum was started by curator Carole Kaye, a grandmother whose fascination with anything teeny has resulted in 14,000 square feet of displays. (Be warned: She started out to build a lone doll house as an innocent diversion.)

A few noteworthy structures include the Roman Forum, a display featuring 52 temples and shrines, and King Tutankhamen's Tomb, complete with mummified king and treasures. All are of the "How did they do that?" variety, and some, such as the Titanic replica made from 75,000 toothpicks, are almost certain to inspire budding artisans to ask, "Mom, can I try that at home?" By and large, however, these are delicate creations. Fortunately, everything is safely ensconced behind Plexiglas so you need not live in fear that one errant swipe of a little hand could result in a large pile of tiny rubble.

**KID-FRIENDLY EATS** If you drive about 10 minutes, you'll find many cute neighborhood-style eateries along Larchmont Boulevard. One kid favorite is **Café Chapeau** (236 Larchmont Blvd., tel. 323/462–4985), where you'll find American breakfast and lunch fare served until 4 PM. If you'd prefer to stay by the museum, try **Marie Callender's** (see the La Brea Tar Pits), a spiffed-up member of the vast chain that features burgers, sandwiches, salads, pizzas, and pastas.

# CASA DE TORTUGA

**58**

You might call Casa de Tortuga (House of Turtles) a hobby that's gotten out of hand. What started with one man's fondness for a couple of turtles turned into a collection of hundreds of these green creatures, so many he had to build a separate structure to house them all.

Walter Allen's preoccupation with turtles has become a tourist treasure. A quirky animal habitat dedicated to the preservation of shelled creatures big and small, Casa de Tortuga is certainly a novel wonder in the world of animal attractions, if only for the surprise of finding out just how many different species of turtle actually exist—about 220 for anyone keeping a tally.

A tour literally takes you through Allen's backyard. On display are hundreds of specimens he's picked up through his world travels. Beyond just your aquarium-variety water turtles and box turtles (the two types commonly found at pet shops), there are also red-eared sliders, Burmese, Sulcatas, and Russian tortoises. Pieces of erroneous turtle lore are intriguingly dispelled along the way. Some turtles (desert turtles, for example) live nowhere near water, and anyone

**KEEP IN MIND** Because the Casa is in a residential area, Allen restricts tours to once daily, so as not to disturb the neighbors. Drop-ins are not accommodated; you are given the address when you call for a reservation. Though small groups may be quickly accommodated on a weekday, you'll have to plan way ahead—perhaps months ahead—for a Saturday. Ask about the annual open house, usually in August or September, when no reservation is required. Children should be reminded not to touch the turtles; though there's no minimum age, the tour is recommended for children school aged and older.

brought up on the "Tortoise and the Hare" legend will be shocked at the speed at which some of the big guys can travel.

Your children will no doubt be awed by the displays, especially by those of the giant species, which live in structures larger than a typical dog house. Be prepared for the inevitable exit question: "Mom, can I get a turtle?" Many kids, and parents, do leave with visions of turtles dancing in their heads. But Casa staff are quick to provide reality checks, such as the fact that all turtles need to be housed outside. Casa does provide "adoption" services to qualified individuals and helps kids understand the care and feeding of these guys through activity and coloring pages provided on the way out.

**KID-FRIENDLY EATS** You may have to wait, but the **Rainforest Cafe** (3333 Bristol St., Costa Mesa, tel. 714/424-9200), with its Animatronic animals, talking trees, and large menu (but no turtle soup!), is a kick for kids. The gimmick at **Planet Hollywood** (1641 W. Sunflower St., Santa Ana, tel. 714/434-7827) is—appropriately—Tinseltown decor.

**HEY, KIDS!** Make sure to tell your friends about the three Aldabra tortoises here, one of which was donated by Michael Jackson. The largest breed of tortoise, these giants can grow to be about 650 pounds and live to be a couple of hundred years old. Thinking about breeding your own family of Aldabras? That can be pretty complicated, since you can't tell the difference between the males and the females until they reach adulthood.

# CATALINA ISLAND

Half the fun of visiting this lovely island off the southern California coast is getting here. Modern boats make the scenic one- to two-hour cruise from Long Beach (among other ports) a pleasure; if you're lucky, you might see a school of dolphins swimming by or, during the winter months, a pod of California gray whales on their annual migration.

Once you're on Catalina (officially Santa Catalina Island), you'll find it a world removed from the bustle of Los Angeles. Although your first glimpse upon landing is of the quaint and thriving seaport town of Avalon, roughly ¾ of this splendid adventure land is in its natural state, making it ideal for exploration.

First, decide on a mode of transportation. Cars are permitted here by permit only, so you'll have to leave yours at home. Options include bikes, golf carts, taxis, and—dare we suggest it!—even walking. Avalon, in fact, is laid out in particularly user-friendly fashion, making hoofing a delightful way to get around.

**KID-FRIENDLY EATS** The **Busy Bee** (306 Crescent Ave., tel. 310/510–1983) serves salads, burgers, and such at umbrella tables overlooking the bay. **Antonio's** (114 Sumner Ave., tel. 310/510–0060) is a funky place for pizza and pasta.

**KEEP IN MIND** Rent bikes from Brown's Bike (107 Pebbly Beach Rd., tel. 310/510–0986), golf carts from Cartopia Golf Cart Rentals (Crescent Ave. and Metropole St., tel. 310/510–2493), and horses from Catalina Stables (600 Avalon Canyon Rd., tel. 310/510–0478). Contact Discovery Tours (tel. 310/510–8687) or Adventure Tours (tel. 310/510–2888) for land, glass-bottom boat, or semisubmersible tours; Catalina Ocean Rafting (tel. 310/510–0211) for raft tours; and Descanso Beach Ocean Sports (tel. 310/510–1226) or Wet Spot Rentals (tel. 310/510–2229) for kayaks and kayak tours.

 Catalina Island Visitors Bureau, Box 217, Avalon 90704

 Free

310/510–1520

Boats usually 9–4, later June–Aug

All ages

Strolling among Avalon's many shops and restaurants is an itinerary mainstay. Further land explorations can be made via one- to four-hour open-tram tours. Shorter jaunts give you a general lay of the land, whereas longer trips reveal some of the island's more unusual aspects, such as the thriving herd of bison, brought over by a film crew in the 1920s and left to roam free. You might also opt for a trip on horseback. A few operators offer ocean raft and kayak tours; in addition to paddling through caves and interesting coves, you may spy a bald eagle or two.

Undersea sights are plentiful as well. Catalina is well known as a haven for snorkelers and scuba divers. For underwater scenery without spoiling your good hair day, try either a glass-bottom boat or semisubmersible tour, both available at Lover's Cove. But however you go, go!

**TRANSPORTATION** From Long Beach, Catalina Cruises (tel. 800/228–2546) offers high-speed ($35 adults, $25 children 2–11) and standard service ($25 adults, $20 children). Catalina Express (tel. 310/519–1212) has high-speed service ($38 adults, $28.50 children 3–11) from Long Beach, San Pedro, and Dana Point. Catalina Passenger Service (tel. 949/673–5245) runs from Newport Beach ($36 adults, $20 children 12 and under). Fares quoted are round-trip, and reservations are a must.

# CHILDREN'S MUSEUM LA HABRA

This comfortable and unassuming children's museum in a renovated 1923 train depot really lets kids go to town. Bright and cheery, the place has no shortage of things to do, and you may well end up having to drag your kids away from the action at the end of the day.

Though seemingly small from the outside, the museum seems to go on forever, with rooms extending out from either side of the entrance. Your children, however, may have trouble making it past the first room, where a Dino Dig pit is the perfect site for excavation and a gas station lets them "fill 'er up" just like a grown-up. In fact, the pump sports price and gallon meters that really run. Your youngsters will thank you for paying the electric bill after pedaling the foot-powered generator. The harder they pedal, the more bulbs they light, but lighting them all takes a *lot* of effort.

Other rooms feature a city bus (the front third of a real one), a well-stocked grocery store, an old-time switchboard, and a fully furnished dollhouse. Train enthusiasts can toot the whistle

**HEY, KIDS!** A sign near the train set shows you the meaning of various whistles, used by engineers to communicate from trains to stations. One short toot means stop. Two long toots mean proceed. Four short toots mean HELP! See if you can use the toy train's whistle to "talk" like an engineer.

on the elaborate model train set; be sure to ask about tours of the antique caboose (outside in the train yard) that take place hourly. An indoor "nature walk" lets your children check out a beehive in operation and pet the fur of an impressive collection of taxidermic animals, including bears, elk, mountain lions, and a coyote.

Future movie stars can get ready for their close-up in the museum's impressive Kids on Stage section, featuring the largest dress-up area most children have ever seen, a piano, microphone, a glamorous stage, and a technical booth from which kids can operate the stage lights. Beyond that is the Preschool Playpark with a tree house for climbing, as well as sturdy plastic toys, including trucks and a play kitchen and tables. What else could a child possibly need?

## KID-FRIENDLY EATS

**Marie Callender's** (340 Whittier Blvd., tel. 562/691–0705) serves the chain's dependable fare of family favorites: burgers, salads, pastas, and pizzas. The selection at **Applebee's** (1238 W. Imperial Hwy., tel. 562/690–0779) isn't as vast, but the restaurant has tasty appetizers, salads, sandwiches, and entrées. Seasonal specialties give the menu spice.

## KEEP IN MIND

If you want to have the museum all to yourself, plan to come during off hours. The quietest times are weekdays after 2, when school groups have gone home. Saturdays are almost always crowded, but often with good reason; the museum offers special events—storytelling, art workshops, and puppet theater—two or three Saturdays each month.

# CHILDREN'S MUSEUM OF LOS ANGELES

A nyone who thinks there's nothing fun for kids to do in downtown Los Angeles is in for a big surprise. With 17,000 square feet of activities, L.A.'s children's museum is fun with a capital "F."

Fifteen exhibits cram activity into every corner. Draw and spin your own moving pictures in the zoetrope, cure your teddy in Take Care of Yourself, or leave your impression in the Shadow Box. The City Streets section features motorcycles to climb on, a gas station, and a truck, and there's plenty of room for riders on the City Streets' bus—the front third of a real L.A. commuter vehicle. As a bonus, the driver gets to operate the passenger doors, and riders can actually pull the "stop" cord, though thankfully, it's been disconnected! Another kid favorite is the full firefighter regalia at the Fire Station.

For role-playing with an L.A. twist, head to the Recording Studio, where your kids can become rock stars, and digital equipment allows them to sing and mix their own music.

## HEY, KIDS!
To remember all the fun you have in the Recording Studio or VideoZone, why not preserve your performance on tape? Just ask Mom or Dad to buy a tape here ($1 each) or bring your own.

**KID-FRIENDLY EATS** For a good, quick bite, try **Leon's Kitchen** (201 N. Los Angeles St., tel. 213/613–0747), located on the ground floor of the museum's building. For off-site—and more interesting—food, try the restaurants of nearby Olvera Street, where you can get tasty Mexican cuisine at places like **La Golondrina** (*see* Olvera Street). Eateries in Little Tokyo are also well within reach.

 310 N. Main St.

 $5 ages 2 and up

 213/687–8800

Mid-June–mid-Sept, M–F 11:30–4, Sa–Su 10–5; mid-Sept–mid-June, Sa–Su 10–5; subject to change

2–10

If they prefer drama, they can create their own radio show with the studio's supply of sound effects tools and musical instruments. In the VideoZone, kids can play TV personality and choose from multiple backdrops thanks to the magic of "blue screen" technology. They can further exercise their creative muscles in the art section, where museum staff members direct craft projects that kids create from donated recycled materials.

A staple since 1979, the children's museum recently made some significant changes. Such stalwart activities as the Lego and Sticky City areas have been removed. Instead, kids can pretend they're space explorers, climbing into a spaceship, operating a miniature remote-controlled land rover, and playing with interplanetary "rocks" on Mars: the Exhibit. If the frenetic pace leaves you in need of some downtime, head to the Corner, where you'll find stacks of the latest children's books and parenting magazines, as well as a wall full of magnetic words waiting for an author.

**TRANSPORTATION** Don't be intimidated by the prospect of parking in the big city. Though the museum is downtown, parking is readily available on site. To reach the parking garage (and the museum), take U.S. 101 and exit at Los Angeles Street. A half block south, turn right into the museum's underground parking garage. The museum itself is located on level four.

# CLUB DISNEY

Your first reaction upon entering might well be, "Why didn't they have this when I was young?"! Disney's entry into the indoor playground market—"For kids and their grownups," as the ads say—is just the kind of indoor play space today's kids pine for, with climbing sculptures, activities, and Disney touches that entertain preschool- and elementary-school-age children.

Disney fans will feel at home here immediately. Though the surrounding shopping plaza was independently designed, the whole place looks like a scene from Disneyland's Main Street USA. The club itself is like a mini theme park, comprising a giant Sorcerer's Apprentice hat surrounded by theme play areas à la Winnie-the-Pooh, Dumbo, and Disney's animated movie of the moment. A craft room allows budding artists to create their own "mousterpieces," and the Mouse Pad (under the sorcerer's hat) contains many computer stations with virtually all the Disney software invented. Older kids can climb to the third story via play sculpture (don't worry; there are stairs, too) and then slide back down. There are also numerous arcade games and a small theater for performances and story time. Though the club was designed to encourage

**HEY, KIDS!** In addition to games, the Mouse Pad features free access to Disney.com and the Daily Blast, Disney's (ordinarily pay-for-play) Internet activity site. Also, be sure to ask about the schedule for the day's events. That way you'll know—and can ask your parents to remember—when you can watch a show in the theater, parade in the Fantasy Fashion Show as your favorite Disney character (costumes provided), or act out a scene from an animated classic.

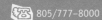
120 S. Westlake Blvd., Westlake Village
Promenade, Westlake Village

805/777-8000

$4.50 adults, $8.50
children 1 and up

T–Th and Su 10–8, F–Sa 10–9

10 and under

parent/child interaction, there are also activities for kids to engage in independently, giving grown-ups a chance to watch (and rest) on the sidelines. Remember, however, that this is not child care, and children cannot be dropped off. Adult supervision is required at all times.

Though Disney has never been known for economical entertainment, Club Disney isn't bad. Admission fees cover all activities, including arcade games, crafts, and computer time—extras at most other indoor playgrounds. You can, however, count on spending at least a few bucks at the adjoining store, whose Disney merchandise rivals most any theme park outlet. On another note, security here is taken seriously. Entering parents and children are fitted with numbered ID bracelets, and no child can leave except with the adult wearing the matching bracelet. It will undoubtedly be *many* hours before your kids are ready to remove those bracelets and go home.

KID-FRIENDLY EATS The **Club Cafe,** right inside Club Disney, offers salads, Mickey-shape pizza, and other convenient lunch food. Out in the Westlake Village Promenade, check out the food court for such eateries as **Noah's Bagels** (140 S. Westlake Blvd., tel. 805/230–2182).

KEEP IN MIND Though only normally open Tuesday through Sunday, the club opens on Monday for major holidays. But watch out! Club Disney is a favorite spot when school is out, so expect crowds during holidays and vacation times. Club Disney is a cool place—literally—so be sure to bring a sweater to account for the extra-efficient air-conditioning. Shoes must be removed upon arrival, but socks are required. And if you live east of Los Angeles, you may want to check out Club Disney's other site, in West Covina (2851 Eastland Center Dr., tel. 626/938–1480).

# DESCANSO GARDENS

When people call Los Angeles a jungle, they're not talking about serene, wooded Descanso, where you can stroll with your kids past fish-filled streams and paths planted with a pleasing collection of flowers and shrubs. A 20-minute drive north from downtown, near Pasadena, the gardens feel utterly insulated from the world outside. Bunnies, squirrels, and ducks scurry (or waddle) about, and koi swim in a tranquil lily pond with stone fish sculptures that spout water from puckered mouths.

No stuffy botanical garden—there's not a KEEP OFF THE GRASS sign in sight—Descanso positively encourages kids to run, not walk, the easy-to-maneuver paths that go uphill, around streams, and through a towering 35-acre oak forest—a rarity in southern California. You can also opt for a guided tram tour. The 160-acre site—vast enough for Walt Disney to have once considered it instead of Anaheim for his theme park—encompasses everything from a bird sanctuary to a Japanese tea garden.

## HEY, KIDS!

Those beautiful flowers in the oak forest, called camellias, are the reason Descanso came to be. The place started as a camellia nursery. Ordinarily only about 8 feet tall, camellias grow to 35 feet here, due largely to their age. Some plants are 60 years old—even older than your parents!

**KEEP IN MIND** Something's always in bloom. Camellias bloom from September to April, tulips and other spring flowers in March and April, and roses from May to December. Descanso's busiest time is mid-March to mid-April, during the Spring Festival of Flowers. The event's special children's nature walks and activities—and the fact that the train runs daily—make this ideal for families; just come during the week or by 10 on weekends to avoid crowds. The popular Christmas festival (with Santa) arrives in early December. All these events make a $65 family membership economical.

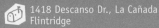 1418 Descanso Dr., La Cañada Flintridge

 818/952-4401

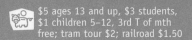 $5 ages 13 and up, $3 students, $1 children 5–12, 3rd T of mth free; tram tour $2; railroad $1.50

 Daily 9–4:30

 All ages

The genus and species of Descanso's multitude of blooms and shrubs probably won't bowl younger children over. "Look, Mommy, pretty flowers!" is about the best you can hope for. Some blooms, including the 5 acres of roses that come out each May, do seem to appeal to even the littlest visitors. But by and large, the bright colors and wide open spaces are the real attention grabbers, enough to make for happy—and tired—campers at the end of the day.

Descanso also has a few kid treats up its sleeve. The Secret Garden in the International Rosarium is a child-size retreat within a retreat, a charming little garden tucked inside a scaled-down hedge maze. It's a private little hideaway for little ones (although the hedges are short enough for you to keep watch from outside). There's also the scale-model Enchanted Railroad (run only on weekends for much of the year), which your youngsters can ride on as it winds through parts of the forest. But it's really only one of many enchanted and enchanting attractions here.

**KID-FRIENDLY EATS** Why not bring a picnic to these beautiful grounds? Alternatively, eat at the on-site **Cafe Court** (tel. 818/952-0219). Though the fare—sandwiches, salads, fruit—is standard, you can't beat the convenience and price. Coloring-book menus and balloons entertain kids at the diner-style **Hill Street Café** (1004 Foothill Blvd., tel. 818/952-1019), where friendly waiters bring tasty, reasonably priced meals: spaghetti, burgers, and corn dogs for kids, chicken, fish, and pasta for adults.

# DISCOVERY MUSEUM OF
## ORANGE COUNTY

M ost parents feel lucky if their kids remember to pick their clothes up off the floor, so many are utterly bemused to watch those same children become rapt in the task of washing towels on a turn-of-the-century washboard. But such is the fun at this historic Santa Ana museum, which features four antique, turn-of-the-century Victorian structures where your children can tinker on long-defunct gadgets to learn about what life was like about a century ago.

Each room in the main building, the 100-plus-year-old Kellogg House (named after its original owner), represents a different theme, most with workable objects of the time. The most popular spot by far is upstairs in the Textile Room, where boys and girls can try on antique finery and learn about those funny-looking knickers and bonnets they'd be sporting if they'd been born just 10 or so decades before. Of course life wasn't all bad. A visit to the home's bathroom reveals that in the days before running bath water, tubs had to be painstakingly filled with water heated on the stove. The result was that people only took a bath once a week.

**HEY, KIDS!** At the working Blacksmith's Shop, you can explore the blacksmith trade of a century ago. Pound an anvil, blow the bellows, or, if you're really lucky, watch the blacksmith of the day work on his latest project. (Blacksmithing demonstrations are guaranteed on the third Sunday of each month but often occur more frequently.) Today's blacksmiths still ply their trade making horseshoes and even repairing large equipment, such as bulldozers. Can you think of other things they might do?

 3101 W. Harvard St., 2 mi from I-405,
Santa Ana

714/540-0404

 $4 ages 13 and up,
$3 children 3–12

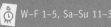 W–F 1–5, Sa–Su 11–3

 3 and up

There are (gasp!) no video games in the Children's Room, but kids seem amply entertained by the electronics-free toys of the time, such as a ticktacktoe board, pickup sticks, a dollhouse, and a sewing machine. Downstairs, the front parlor has a workable Victrola, Edison Talking Machine, pump organ, and hand-crank telephone. In the kitchen, look for, among other things, a butter churn and an old-fashioned stove-top toaster.

There's more activity outside. Spread around the museum's 12-acre property is a nature center, featuring reptiles, bird's nests, and habitat for other animals, as well as a small barnyard area with the usual petting-zoo suspects (sheep, goats, etc.). Brand new is the Eco-Art Gallery, where kids can create masterpieces out of recycled materials (no extra charge). Visiting on a Sunday? Ask about special Sunday activities such as guided nature walks and crafts.

**KID-FRIENDLY EATS** The museum has picnic areas. South Coast Plaza can satisfy everyone's tastes. **Back Bay Rowing and Running Club** (3333 Bristol St., tel. 714/641–0118) has fish, grills, and an enormous (we're talking humongous) salad bar, plus congenial owner Donnie. Across the street is the ever-dependable **Ruby's** (333 Bear St., Costa Mesa, tel. 714/662–7829).

**KEEP IN MIND** The Discovery Museum's goal is to illustrate life in days of yore. With that in mind, many activities are of the gone-but-not-forgotten, quaint, and low-tech variety, such as Children's Teas, which are held on holidays such as Valentine's Day and Easter. The flagship event here is the annual 1890s Market Day, when period-clad actors, as well as participatory crafts, games, and contests, recreate a 19th-century celebration. Check the museum's September schedule for dates.

# DISCOVERY SCIENCE CENTER

This is *not* where Pietro the Human Pincushion defies pain and agony while lying on a bed of nails. It's where you and your children will, discovering not only that it's not at all painful but also why.

This science museum, opened in 1998, gets participants wholly involved in science by doing things like lying on a bed of nails. Your child stretches out on the deceptively smooth wooden table and then pushes a button to raise 3,500 sharp nails painlessly beneath him, thus learning the secret of weight disbursement (and, thankfully, not of acupuncture) and why sitting on a thousand nails hurts so much less that sitting on just one.

Though "hands-on" has become the mantra of virtually all of today's interactive museums, the twist at the 59,000-square-foot Discovery Science Center is the number of so-called body-on activities, exhibits that allow your family to become immersed in the process of learning about science. In addition to lying on nails, you can experience earthquakes of

KID-FRIENDLY EATS Choose between two on-site cuisines at **Taco Bell/Pizza Hut Express** (tel. 714/542–5125). If that's not enough choice, head to the Main Place mall, whose several restaurants include an **Olive Garden** (2800 N. Main St., tel. 714/541–8323).

HEY, KIDS! Are you ready to become an astronaut? Take a look at what future space travelers need to do before countdown. Reaction Time—where you respond to a panel of lights—tests how quick you are. Grip Strength, a self-explanatory test of hand power, is essential for peak space performance. The Manipulator Arm puts you in command—via joystick—of a laser-clad arm, similar to those on space stations. Precision is an astronaut's hallmark. How well can you control its motion?

2500 N. Main St., Santa Ana

714/542-2823

 $9.50 adults, $7.50 children 3–17; 3-D laser show $2

 Daily 10–5

All ages

varying intensities, walk through a tornado, and create your whole-body impression in a wall full of pins, the super-size version of those hand-held gizmos you find at toy stores.

If you'd prefer to keep your body out of it, there's plenty of plain-old hands-on stuff as well, such as the Cloud Ring Maker and an area where you can use wind to create sand dunes. You can even test your readiness for interplanetary travel in the center's Air and Space section. Electronic finger painting, story hours, and crafts are among the activities for kids 5 and under at the KidStation; there's also a soft-play area for the really little ones in your group. And the whole family's bound to like the presentations in the 3-D laser theater.

**TRANSPORTATION** Getting here seems easy, but there are a couple of tricky turns, particularly if you're coming from the north. If you're driving south on I–5, exit at Main Street North. Take your first left onto Santa Clara Avenue and the next left onto Main Street. The science center is on your left. From the south, head north on I–5, also exiting at Main Street North. Turn right off of the ramp onto Main Street. Then take your first left into the parking lot. Keep an eye out for the center's hallmark 10-story cube.

# DISNEYLAND

One of the best things about having a kid is being able to act like one yourself. So though you don't actually need a child to go to Disneyland—solo adults account for a substantial percentage of "guests"—holding a little one's hand legitimizes your own squeals and screeches as you steer around in a flying elephant or speed along in a make-believe rocket ship.

Of course, the really good news is that your children are likely to have an equally splendid time. Commercialism aside, Disneyland is a hoot. If you've got preschoolers, expect to spend much of the day tooling around Fantasyland, where your kids may want to twirl endlessly on the teacups (hot tip: twirl only before lunch). Other must-see Fantasyland fare includes Dumbo the Flying Elephant (notorious for long lines but a must for novice visitors), Snow White's Scary Adventures (too scary for some kids), and Storybook Land Canal Boats (magnificent miniatures you won't find at other Disney parks). The talking mailboxes and other interactive gizmos at Mickey's Toontown turn the village into a living cartoon; you may find it hard to tear your little ones away long enough to enjoy another toddlers'

**HEY, KIDS!** It looks so innocent from the outside, but don't be fooled by Tomorrowland's Cosmic Wave water maze. You *will* get wet—soaked, actually, right down to your sloshing sneaks! Fountains spurt in changing patterns, surprising you repeatedly, so don't expect a route that looks dry to stay that way very long. Once in the center, see if you can figure out the physics behind the enormous ball on the water pedestal. It moves around easily but, inexplicably, never falls off!

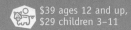

favorite, the Disneyland Railroad, a vintage steam train that chugs through, among other places, a prehistoric dino land.

The park's "mountain" rides (Splash Mountain, Big Thunder Mountain Railroad, Space Mountain, and Matterhorn Bobsleds—roller coasters all), the Indiana Jones Adventure, and Rocket Rods (billed as Disneyland's longest and fastest ride) are more obviously for older kids, if only because of height requirements. As for the other adventures, you'll have to use your discretion. Star Tours (a flight simulator) and even the innocent-looking Jungle Cruise are going to thrill some little ones, terrify others. One show to be wary of with young children is "Honey, I Shrunk the Audience." The 3-D attraction is a blast for older kids, but younger ones are often reduced to tears. The end-of-day don't-miss for the entire family is the nighttime Fantasmic! show on the Rivers of America.

**KID-FRIENDLY EATS** You can find food at vendor carts or cafeteria-style restaurants, or make a reservation (in person upon arrival) at the **Blue Bayou Restaurant.** The **PCH Grill** (Disneyland Pacific Hotel, 1717 West St., tel. 714/999–0990) offers breakfast with Disney characters, delicious Asian-inspired lunches and dinners, and make-your-own pizza that entertains *and* feeds kids.

**KEEP IN MIND** Visit in fall or winter, when attendance is lower and the heat is bearable; remember you'll be in direct sun on many lines. If you live locally, ask about winter pass discounts (usually January–May). You shouldn't budget under a day here. There's *plenty* to do, and it'll take a while to get your money's worth. However, if you visit in summer, get here early and escape at midday, when crowds and heat are at peak levels. Return later to go on rides after little ones have left and for nighttime entertainment and fireworks.

# FIGHTERTOWN

For anyone who wants to fly military maneuvers without enlisting in the Navy, this is the next best thing. A state-of-the-art flight simulator center (similar to those used in military flight school), Fightertown lets aerial daredevil wannabes "fly" missions in authentically re-created military aircraft. A successful mission consists of taxiing, taking off, and landing, preferably in one piece.

Pilots get their "flight orders" in the Fightertown lobby (ostensibly an aircraft carrier), don standard-issue flight suits and helmets, and await their turn in the Fightertown Officer's Club. Before boarding, everyone gets 30 minutes of flight school. Children should pay close attention as they'll have to control altitude, speed, and landing gear. Next, each young pilot climbs into a cockpit and is sealed beneath a canopy, either the familiar clear bubble or a fully enclosed version, depending on the aircraft. Then the adventure begins; images are displayed either on a 12-foot by 12-foot screen or a 30" internal monitor—again, depending on aircraft. A flight instructor in a control tower offers direction throughout,

## KEEP IN MIND
Ask about occasional kids' discounts of up to 50% during the week and on weekend mornings. After you land, if your family's collective adrenaline is pumped up for more action, head to the Sega Gameworks, also in the mall; it's stocked with all the latest Sega games.

**HEY, KIDS!** As a novice, you'll test your mettle in a canyon run. Fly below enemy radar or risk being shot down. Also, keep an eye on enemy ships below; they may be packing artillery. Once the family's gotten some flight experience, challenge Mom or Dad to an aerial dogfight. Can't you just hear yourself apologizing, "I'm really sorry I shot you down, Mom, after all those years you've fed me, clothed me, and taken care of me. I just had to."

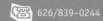   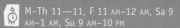

Puente Hills Mall, 1560 S. Azusa Ave., off I-60, City of Industry

626/839-0244

$29.99–$59.99

M–Th 11—11, F 11 AM–12 AM, Sa 9 AM–1 AM, Su 9 AM–10 PM

12 and up

but pilots take note: It is possible to "crash." (One mom crashed five times!) Unlike the real thing, however, you're quickly relaunched.

The novice program includes taxi, takeoff, a canyon bombing run, gunfire from an enemy oil derrick, and landing on an aircraft carrier. Experienced participants move on to more complex runs with barrel rolls and even dogfights, since up to nine jets are aloft at a time.

Pilots choose from five types of aircraft, with price dependent on the bells and whistles. The most expensive—the F-117 Stealth and the F-14 Tomcat—feature full-motion hydraulic simulation. The latter has dual seats and controls, allowing two pilots to share the cockpit and the cost. Another two-seater, the EA-6A Prowler—the cheapest, along with the F-18 Hornet—can accommodate copilots as young as 6. The F-16 is the jet Tom Cruise flew in *Top Gun*. From training through landing, the entire experience lasts about an hour—a very tense and intense, exciting, and unforgettable hour.

KID-FRIENDLY EATS In typical retail-utopia fashion, the Puente Hills Mall has two food courts with fast food as far as the eye can see. To be seated with a menu, try the **Outback Steakhouse** (1418 Azusa Ave., tel. 626/810–6765), which gives you a choice of mammoth platters of beef. You won't find any major surprises at colorful **T.G.I. Friday's** (17427 Colima Rd., tel. 626/839–5044), but the large menu of burgers, sandwiches, and salads is known for its dependability.

# FORT MACARTHUR MILITARY MUSEUM

**W**ar-era attractions don't get much better than this. A rare find overlooking the coast—literature declares it the best-preserved U.S. structure of its kind—this defunct fortress has gun batteries, strategy rooms, and tunnels. But this fascinating piece of modern military history has something else going for it: It's a really cool place to explore.

Built in 1916, Fort MacArthur was the first line of defense against possible invaders off the Pacific Coast. Back then, battleships ranked as the primary war threat, and armed troops stationed here used their vantage point atop the bluff to scope out incoming ships. Pacific Coast threats loomed particularly large early in the century, climaxing at the beginning of World War II, when submarine sightings and red alerts rang out regularly.

There was also a time when an underground fortress was planned, but though many tunnels were drawn up, only a few were built. Children enjoy hunting around for the tunnel that connects the front of the fortress to the back. But make sure to accompany your youngsters, as it can be creepy in that dark space.

**KEEP IN MIND** For more military history, check out the restored S.S. *Lane Victory*, (Berth 94, under the Vincent Thomas Bridge, tel. 310/519–9545), a WWII cargo ship featuring tours and memorabilia. In nearby Wilmington, the 1864 Banning Residence Museum (401 E. Main St., tel. 310/548–7777), home to General Phineas Banning, a founder of Los Angeles, features tours of its mansion, a one-room schoolhouse, and a stagecoach barn, and the Drum Barracks Civil War Museum (1052 N. Banning Blvd., tel. 310/548–7509) is the only Civil War–era army building remaining in southern California.

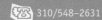 3601 S. Gaffey St., I–110 south to Angels
Gate Park, San Pedro

 310/548–2631

 Donations requested

 T, Th, and Sa–Su 12–5

All ages

Eventually, the passage of time and the advent of military aircraft made such posts obsolete. Fort MacArthur became Los Angeles's air defense headquarters in the 1950s, home to more than a dozen short-range missiles. By 1974, Fort MacArthur had had its day as a military installation, but as a museum, it's now come into its own. Music of the 1930s plays throughout, photos and a video presentation document its history, and many rooms appear as they did in the facility's heyday. The austere, cement structure is both a chilling reminder of World War II threats and a chilly respite from L.A. heat, even on the hottest summer days. The climb to the top of the two gun batteries—guns have been removed, so you'll have to use your imagination—is indeed steep, but the spectacular view will explain why this site was chosen in the first place. Military reenactments are held the weekend following the Fourth of July.

**HEY, KIDS!** The weapons are gone, but their legacy lives on. The seacoast guns that once occupied these heavy-duty batteries were capable of firing 14 miles out to sea. Despite their mammoth size, these specimens of artillery were handled adeptly by experts who could load, fire, and retract in less than 20 seconds.

**KID-FRIENDLY EATS** The too-cute **Ports O' Call Village** (Sampson Way, tel. 310/547–9977), resembling a New England fishing hamlet, features cobblestone paths and lots of eating and shopping. The **Whale & Ale** (327 W. 7th St., tel. 310/832–0363), a favorite among longshoremen and families alike, has jolly old English food and such American staples as prime rib and grilled cheese. The **Busy Bee Market** (2413 S. Walker St., tel. 310/832–8660) makes some of the best sandwiches in town—including a to-die-for pork sandwich.

# GETTY CENTER

If you're looking for a welcoming place to introduce your kids to art and its appreciation, look no further than the Getty Center. Though admittedly renowned more for its architecture (an airy, contemporary, Richard Meier–designed structure featuring lots of glass and marble) than its art collection (spanning 600 years of sculpture, manuscripts, photography, paintings, and, most notably, decorative art, such as furniture), the grand Getty is an especially good first museum. In fact, designers and programmers took great pains to incorporate younger visitors into the museum's repertoire.

You can rent audio guides, personal digital players with kid-friendly prerecorded tours that are recommended for parents, too—to spur dialogue among families. Also look for four Art Information (AI) rooms: one in each art pavilion. AI rooms have touch-screen computer stations where you and your children can go on a virtual venture through the museum and learn about many artworks. Knowledgeable docents can embellish what's in the computer and point you toward the collections. Aspiring artists can even try their hand at easels, with

## HEY, KIDS!

The center's marble—one million square feet of it—was brought over from Italy. Virtually every one of the 300,000 pieces on floors and walls has a cool little fossil embedded in it: leaves, flowers, and occasionally a small animal. How many can you find?

**KEEP IN MIND** Though admission is free, it costs $5 to park, and you'll need a reservation to do so. You may have heard that lots are booked well into the future, but it's not impossible to get a space. The frenzy surrounding the museum has cooled some, and weekday spaces—and even some weekends—are sometimes available on short notice. If you don't bring a car—you can get dropped off or take a cab or bus—you don't need a reservation at all. Just call on the day you plan to visit to make sure lines aren't snaking out the door.

still-life subjects set up on tables.

Where the Getty really shines, however, is in its Family Room. Here youngsters can try on costumes corresponding to the attire worn in famous paintings—perhaps Edwardian duds— check themselves out in the mirror, and then, after removing the clothes, find the corresponding artwork in the galleries. They can explore the art of posing, "try on a new face" via masks, or, as some toddlers do, take a (parent-supervised!) nap. Docents present impromptu demonstrations. Sign out one of the inventive game boxes, offering activities, such as a museum treasure hunt, that teach kids about the collections while they have fun. The museum also features regular family programs, such as storytelling and workshops, as well as quarterly family festivals with music and dance. If your kids need a break from art appreciation, there's plenty of open space and lovely gardens perfect for strolling. If all that fails to make an impression, the tram ride up the mountain will make kids feel they're at Disneyland.

**KID-FRIENDLY EATS** Eating on site is very convenient. Choices include the self-service **cafés,** all of which have indoor and outdoor seating as well as such kid-favorite food as pizza and hot dogs. The full-service **Restaurant** (tel. 310/440-7300) features some stellar views and its own original artwork, as well as salads, grilled items, and daily specials that appeal to more grown-up palates. Reservations are recommended. If you'd prefer to bring your own, the Getty allows you to dine alfresco in its picnic area.

# GRIFFITH OBSERVATORY

ike many Los Angeles attractions, this planetarium and science center is notable for its celebrity as much as its function. Featured in a scene from the James Dean film *Rebel Without a Cause* and in numerous movie and television productions since, Griffith is one of the most recognized science structures in the country. And no wonder. In addition to its merit as a science center, it has a prime location—high atop a hill in L.A.'s Griffith Park, with incredible views of Los Angeles and the fabled Hollywood sign. The drive up alone makes it worth a visit.

Celestial enthusiasts will be happy to know that Griffith Observatory is more than just a pretty face. Filled with exhibits and activities to learn about meteorites, stars, and the earth, the observatory is a great place to take the family on an exploration of the universe. Along with a Zeiss telescope in the famed dome (available for viewing on clear nights), there are samples of space debris hurled to earth and activities to test your children's (and your) knowledge of the universe, constituting a Constellation Quiz. You can even try your hand at creating

**HEY, KIDS!** Tired of being a kid? Use the Astro Computer to calculate your age in interplanetary years. You'd feel grown up (roughly four times as old) on Mercury, which travels around the sun four times—in other words, four of its years—in the time it takes the earth to go around just once. On the other hand, even your 90-year-old grandma would be young (3, to be exact) on Saturn, which takes 30 of our years to revolve around the sun once.

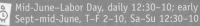
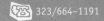

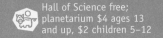

2800 E. Observatory Rd., off Los Feliz Blvd. or Vermont Ave.

323/664–1191

Hall of Science free; planetarium $4 ages 13 and up, $2 children 5–12

Mid-June–Labor Day, daily 12:30–10; early Sept–mid-June, T–F 2–10, Sa–Su 12:30–10

5 and up

your own earthquake—a dubious activity in this region. Weight watchers will be delighted to learn what they'd weigh if they lived on the moon (⅙ of their weight here). On the other hand, if you've cheated on the diet this week, you'll want to skip the feature that tells you what you'd weigh on Jupiter.

In addition to its popular Lasarium shows, the planetarium at Griffith offers space exploration daily. Shows here are less of the snooze variety than at some other places, although those expecting an ultraslick extravaganza might be disappointed. Griffith's version is truly educational, but a live scientist cum narrator is comical enough to be make it entertaining as well. After all, this is L.A.

**KID-FRIENDLY EATS** The parking lot **snack bar** serves vending machine–quality food. Better bets are to bring a picnic or try a Hollywood eatery. The **House of Pies Restaurant and Bakery** (1869 N. Vermont Ave., tel. 323/666–9961) has a huge coffee shop–style menu, all-day breakfast, and 34 kinds of pie (the big seller: French Strawberry Cream).

**KEEP IN MIND** Though children of all ages are allowed into the exhibits, those 4 and under are barred from most planetarium shows. However, the afternoon show in summer (usually at 1:30) is geared for kids and permits children under 5. Nighttime, particularly in the summer, can bring crowds and parking woes. Plan to arrive at least an hour early if you want to attend either a planetarium or Lasarium show. And be forewarned: Expect long lines any time the Zeiss telescope is available for public viewing.

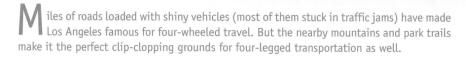

# GRIFFITH PARK HORSE RENTAL

Miles of roads loaded with shiny vehicles (most of them stuck in traffic jams) have made Los Angeles famous for four-wheeled travel. But the nearby mountains and park trails make it the perfect clip-clopping grounds for four-legged transportation as well.

Riding the Los Angeles range is something both novice and veteran equestrians can do, and the easiest place to get in the saddle is at Griffith Park Horse Rental. Located in Los Angeles's famed and vast park, the stable offers one- to two-hour jaunts that make forays into the hills, revealing spectacular views. Unlike many area stables, the one at Griffith offers unguided as well as guided tours, so experienced riders (as well as brave-but-foolish souls) can meander out into the wilds on their own. Guides cost a little more, but beginners take heed: Even if the ranchers don't spot your inexperience, the horses probably will. Old Trigger can become a mite stubborn under a beginner, so you're advised to mosey with folks who know what they're doing. In addition to ensuring that you don't get lost, guides can point out pertinent sights along the way.

**KEEP IN MIND** Riders should wear closed-toe shoes, and long pants are advised, especially for long rides. If you're brand new to the saddle, start with a shorter ride or you (and your lower half!) may live to regret it. For riding opportunities in other areas, try Adventures in Horseback (tel. 818/706–0888), in Malibu; Two Winds Ranch (tel. 805/498–9222), in Newbury Park; or Country Horse Trails (tel. 714/538–5860), at Irvine Regional Park.

Los Angeles Equestrian Center, 480
Riverside Dr., off I-5, Burbank

818/840-8401

$15/hr, guide $5/hr extra;
BBQ ride $40; picnic ride
$50; Autry tour $60

M–F 8–7, Sa–Su 8–5

6 and up

If you're up for a short ride, head up on the Skyline trail where, if it's a clear day, you can see the entire San Fernando Valley. Longer rides can take you as far as Dante's View, where you'll see the Griffith Park Observatory as well as downtown Los Angeles.

Those who plan ahead can opt for one of the stable's picnic rides (reservations required), 3½-hour trips that include a visit to Amir's Garden, a beautiful expanse of flowers above the valley, and a picnic lunch for you and your horse about halfway through. On alternate Friday nights, the stable hosts BBQ rides that include a 1½-hour guided ride and a barbecue dinner upon return. They start at 6:30 and are available on a first-come, first-served basis. The five-hour Autry tour includes, fittingly enough, entrance to the Gene Autry museum.

KID-FRIENDLY EATS  After a ride in Griffith Park, try Island's (117 W. Broadway, Glendale, tel. 818/545–3555) for burgers, sandwiches, and tacos in a colorful tropical atmosphere. Just a short trot from the equestrian center, **Viva Fresh** (900 Riverside Dr., tel. 818/845–2425) serves Mexican favorites such as burritos, tacos, and enchiladas.

# HOLLYWOOD BOWL

There is more to children's music than Raffi, Barney, and the latest adolescent teenie-bopper quintet. You just have to know where to look. One place is the Hollywood Bowl, which has been introducing children and their parents to different kinds of music for more than three decades. Here you can warm up to classical, jazz, blues, and more, all presented in family-friendly concerts aimed at making music appreciaters of us all.

A cultural landmark, the Hollywood Bowl offers an annual Open House, a six-week program featuring a different performer and style of music each week. Past summers have showcased African drum music, Latin jazz, and southern blues, among others. These outdoor events—held not in the main theater but in the box-office area—have a festival feel. Afterwards, kids can take part in related crafts. After a program of southern music, for example, kids created a paper quilt. Occasionally, as was the case after the African drum concert, children can try their hands on instruments similar to those used in the concert.

**KEEP IN MIND** In winter, the Philharmonic's family concerts move indoors and downtown to the Dorothy Chandler Pavilion (Music Center of Los Angeles County, 135 N. Grand Ave. 323/850–2000). Called Symphonies for Youth, the seven Saturday-morning concerts ($8–$10 each) feature such works as *The Magic Flute* and Ravel's *Mother Goose Suite*. All concerts have a celebrity MC. For 45 minutes before performances, the lobby overflows with activities.

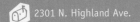 2301 N. Highland Ave.

 323/850-2000

 Open House $3 performance, $1 crafts; Family Concert varies, children 12 and under usually ½ adult price

 Open House early July–mid-Aug, M–F; Family Concerts about 1/mth, 7:30

Open House 3 and up, Family Concert 8 and up

Three orchestras (all under the Los Angeles Philharmonic's umbrella) call the Hollywood Bowl's main amphitheater home in summer: the main Philharmonic orchestra, which gives adult-oriented concerts on Tuesday and Thursday nights; the Clayton-Hamilton Jazz Orchestra; and the Hollywood Bowl Orchestra, which offers three Family Concerts each season. For a classical freebie, stop by the Hollywood Bowl on a summer Tuesday or Thursday morning; you may get to see the Philharmonic in rehearsal.

Naturally, the choice of music for youth concerts takes young tastes into account, but the format isn't patronizing. In fact, Open House performers are chosen for their educational performance background as well as musicianship, and concerts are entertaining *and* instructive. It's like introducing your children to a new vegetable: You can make them try a bite, but they're more likely to really like it if you disguise it as something else.

**KID-FRIENDLY EATS** Fans of alfresco dining may want to pack their own picnic. Not too far away are the eateries and people-watching of **Universal Studios CityWalk** (*see* Warner Bros. Studios Tour). Everything from ordinary burgers to penne with pine nuts is available at the **Daily Grill** (12050 Ventura Blvd., Studio City, tel. 818/769–6336).

**HEY, KIDS!** After an Open House concert, ask Mom and Dad to bring you into the main amphitheater, an awesome concert venue, especially if the Philharmonic is rehearsing. Take a peek at the Hollywood Bowl Museum, where you can learn about this historic open shell and the people who've played here—everyone from the Beatles to Hanson.

# HOLLYWOOD ENTERTAINMENT MUSEUM

**43**

Families with an affinity for all things *Star Trek* or *Cheers* will find much to delight them at one of the newer tourist attraction on this popular stretch of Hollywood Boulevard. Through tours, exhibits, artifacts, and hands-on activities, the museum offers entertainment enthusiasts a glimpse into Hollywood past and present, including the "final frontier" and a little place "where everybody knows your name."

Act One of your visit begins in the museum's main gallery with an elaborate, six-minute film montage featuring clips of the classics. The film is entertaining not only for its visual beauty (it was pieced together by an Oscar-winning filmmaker), but also for the challenge it poses as you try to name all the films and actors that flash across the giant screens. The main gallery also includes interactive exhibits where you can explore the craft of movie making—from makeup artistry to character development—and tinker with touch-screen computers that explore film history and challenge your knowledge of celluloid lore. In the adjoining Education Center for the Entertainment Arts, tour guides lead editing and Foley (sound

## HEY, KIDS!

Sit on Norm and Cliff's bar stools and hunt for the signatures *Cheers* cast members carved in the bar. Trekkies can see the bridge doors from the original *Star Trek* (unfortunately, they won't open as you approach) and read what those scribbles in the *Enterprise*'s engineering "corridor" really say.

## KEEP IN MIND

This relatively undiscovered, uncrowded gem is a fairly quick visit, two hours max. Other entertainment on the boulevard includes the Hollywood Walk of Fame, Hollywood Guinness World of Records (6764 Hollywood Blvd., tel. 323/463–6433), Hollywood Wax Museum (6767 Hollywood Blvd., tel. 323/462–5991), Frederick's of Hollywood Lingerie Museum (6608 Hollywood Blvd., tel. 323/466–8506), and the historic Hollywood Roosevelt Hotel (7000 Hollywood Blvd., tel. 323/466–7000), whose photo gallery documents Hollywood's Golden Age.

7021 Hollywood Blvd., Hollywood

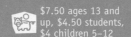 $7.50 ages 13 and up, $4.50 students, $4 children 5-12

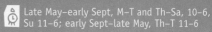 Late May–early Sept, M–T and Th–Sa, 10–6, Su 11–6; early Sept–late May, Th–T 11–6

323/465-7900

 5 and up

effects) demonstrations, allowing a few lucky volunteers to try their hand at putting sound effects to film. It's harder than it looks!

For many, however, the highlight of a visit here is the trip "backstage" to tour the museum's "back lot." You'll see original costumes and props from such film and television productions as *The Coneheads* and *Happy Days*. Your family can amble through a couple of familiar places, including the bridge and transporter room from *Star Trek: The Next Generation,* as well as the entire bar set from *Cheers*. Both sets feature computer touch screens, where you can engage in *Star Trek* trivia or take a look back at some classic *Cheers* scenes.

*KID-FRIENDLY EATS* **Hamburger Hamlet** (6914 Hollywood Blvd., tel. 323/467–6106), across the street from the museum, serves hamburgers, salads, sandwiches, steaks, and other typical chain-restaurant fare. Ask about discounts sometimes offered with museum passes. **Shelly's Café** (7013 Hollywood Blvd., tel. 323/467–2233), next door to the museum, is a neighborhood comfort-food place known among locals for its hamburgers, fried chicken, fried shrimp, and sandwiches.

# THE HUNTINGTON

Its full name is the Huntington Library, Art Collections, and Botanical Gardens, and different people come for different reasons, taking in any or all of its three facets. But whatever your family decides to come for, the Huntington has a lot to offer. Even if none of the cultural offerings appeal to the littlest ones in the family, the institution's surprisingly liberal and unstuffy philosophy—that its sprawling grounds should be used for "cartwheeling, shrieking and releasing boundless energy"—is bound to be a hit.

Though the atmosphere alone is inviting, the cultural wares here are impressive as well. Founded by businessman Henry E. Huntington, the facility showcases its progenitor's mind-boggling personal collection of art and rare books, including Gainsborough's *Blue Boy*, an original Gutenberg Bible, and a collection of early editions of Shakespeare, to name a few. More than 100 acres of gardens include a 12-acre desert garden, a lavish rose garden, a tropical jungle garden, and a Japanese garden. The last features a drum bridge as well as a traditional Japanese house, the walls of which slide open to afford a peek inside; entry, however, is forbidden.

**HEY, KIDS!** The koi ponds have been around since the turn of the century, when Mr. Huntington decided to create his own personal oasis. Generations of turtles—many diamond-back terrapins—have lived here, and many of the current crop are descendants of those who roamed during the Huntingtons' time. Baby ducklings are also known to waddle along the banks. As for the koi themselves, make sure to look for "koi chow" dispensers, so you can actually feed them.

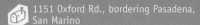

1151 Oxford Rd., bordering Pasadena, San Marino

626/405–2141, 626/405–2127 special programs

$8.50 adults, $6 students 12 and up, 1st Th of mth free

June–Aug, T–Su 10:30–4;30; Sept–May, T–F 12–4:30, Sa–Su 10:30–4:30

All ages, summer program 5–12

Organizers here have taken great pains to include children, not just tolerate them. Inside the library and galleries, staff members promote creative ways for children to explore the art and books—perhaps by comparing today's style of dress to what's shown in some paintings or by ambling the mansion, now a gallery, that was once home to Mr. Huntington and his wife. Outside, Plant Discovery Carts help your kids learn about the greenery, while the "Explore!" family guide helps steer your brood through the entire facility. And when your children have had enough of learning about art and literature and nature, you can just relax and watch the abundant small wildlife: ducks and turtles, koi and frogs.

**KID-FRIENDLY EATS** English tea (frilly dresses optional) is served in the **Rose Garden Tea Room** (tel. 626/683–8131), while the **Rose Garden Café** serves sandwiches. **Johnny Rockets** (16 Miller Alley, Pasadena, tel. 626/793–6570) delivers burgers in '50s style, and **Russell's Restaurant** (30 N. Fair Oaks Ave., Pasadena, tel. 626/578–1404) dishes up tasty home cooking.

**KEEP IN MIND** In addition to daily activities, the Huntington offers free nature crafts on the first Saturday of every month from 1 to 3; no reservations are required. Monthly Children's Garden Workshops, hosted on Saturdays, present different projects each month; past workshops have included flower arranging, bread baking, and papermaking. Reservations and an extra fee, usually around $12 per child, are required. Elementary schoolkids can take part in weeklong summer programs.

# IRVINE REGIONAL PARK

**4 1**

You want to go for a bike ride; the kids want to get on a horse or pony. On those days when you're looking for a place to make everybody happy, try this sprawling park that combines nature with novelty. Here a vast resource of outdoor activities paired with a handful of attractions will make your children feel like they've happened on a kind of amusement park in the woods.

At 477 acres, Irvine provides a lot of territory to cover, which you can do on bike or on foot along miles of hiking and biking trails that entwine the park. Playground equipment makes perfect pit stops for swinging and sliding.

However, it's the center of the park where all the action is, including pony rides and a scale-model train that chugs passengers on a 1-mile loop around a section of the park. Near the train station, at Country Trails Horse Rentals, you can try an even earlier form of

## HEY, KIDS!
The mewing you hear isn't a cat stuck in a tree; it's a peacock. The birds were brought to the park in the 1970s, and today 50 or so roam freely here, surprising visitors who think they've escaped from a cage. If you're lucky, you may see a male displaying his colorful tail.

**KEEP IN MIND** The open hours of the attractions within the park vary throughout the year, sometimes changing without notice. Many places are open daily in the summer but only on weekends the rest of the year. It's best to call ahead to confirm times (tel. 760/956–8441 pony rides, 714/997–3968 train, 714/633–2022 zoo, 714/289–9616 nature center, 714/538–5860 horseback riding, 714/997–3656 pedal boats). Horseback rides, generally geared to the novice, are typically offered Wednesday through Sunday; reservations are required.

 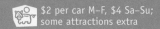 

1 Irvine Park Rd., north end of
Jamboree Rd., Orange

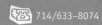 714/633-8074

$2 per car M–F, $4 Sa–Su;
some attractions extra

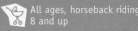 Daily 7–6 (to 9 Apr–Oct). Nature center Sa–Su 11–3:45

All ages, horseback riding 8 and up

transportation on one- to three-hour guided horseback tours around the park. A small lake, also in the heart of the park, accommodates anglers as well as pedal boats.

One of the park's real surprises is the small but steadily growing 3-acre Orange County Zoo, home to such native southwestern animals as a black bear, a mountain lion, bobcats, coyotes, armadillos, porcupines, and even a bald eagle and a golden eagle.

More than 100 years old, Irvine Regional Park qualifies as the oldest regional park in the state. You'll learn that fact, along with other information about the park's history and the plants and animals that live here, at the on-site nature center, near the zoo. And you probably will have satisfied your family's varied interests along the way.

**KID-FRIENDLY EATS** The park was once used by pioneers as a picnic ground, and not a whole lot has changed. You'll find no shortage of places to picnic here. For burgers, hot dogs, and snacks, try the **snack bar** near the lake. For children's favorites as well as some good food—homemade right down to the soups, gravies, and mashed potatoes—try the **Katella Family Grill** (1325 W. Katella Ave., tel. 714/997–9191).

# KIDSEUM

On a typical day at this half of a two-part institution (the Bowers Museum of Cultural Art is a couple of doors down), the staff and its visitors were fully immersed in a South Pacific family festival with leis, hula dancing, and all. Needless to say, everyone was having a ball (or should we say a luau?). Such special events occur one Saturday a month at this inventive multicultural learning and play center, where kids can get in on activities (such as those hula-dancing lessons), storytelling, and other endeavors geared to the month's cultural theme.

But don't miss out on the Kidseum's standard fare; the everyday stuff is worth a visit as well. Bright and colorful spaces are strewn with games and play areas. Among the favorites is the well-stocked dress-up area; it literally overflows with garb. The mix-and-match wardrobe of sombreros, Indian saris, Chinese gowns, Colonial dresses, and Dutch wooden shoes, to name just a few, makes for some pretty eccentric ensembles. Kids can keep the clothes on as they step through the door to the Time Vault (once the bank vault of this old financial building)

**HEY, KIDS!** Make sure to ask about the daily craft that corresponds to the facility's monthly ethnic theme. During the South Pacific festival, for example, kids got to make their own fresh-flower leis. Imagine what you can make when you go!

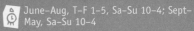
and take a seat in the stagecoach or saddle (a wooden horse), or have a go at grinding some corn. Crafts, also based on the theme of the month, can be undertaken whenever the museum is open, and the puppet theater area is filled with favorite animal "performers." For less stimulation, there's a quiet book corner for curling up with a good story.

Though indeed well stocked, the Kidseum is small and intimate enough not to be overwhelming. The staff is particularly amiable, allowing kids to fully explore their imaginations. Noted one smiling worker observing the activity, "As you can see, we're not worried about the kids being neat and tidy."

**KID-FRIENDLY EATS** The full-service **Topaz Cafe** (2002 N. Main St., tel. 714/835–2002), right inside the Bowers Museum, dishes up creative world cuisine plus a traditional children's menu. **California Pizza Kitchen** (*see* the Santa Ana Zoo at Prentice Park), at the Main Place shopping center, serves the obvious fare.

**KEEP IN MIND** The Kidseum admission fee also covers entrance to the nearby Bowers Museum (2002 N. Main St., tel. 714/567–3600), where you can get a look at some amazing ethnic art and artifacts from around the world. As at the Kidseum, the focus here is on cultural history and multiculturalism, but the Bowers is oriented more to adults.

# KIDSPACE CHILDREN'S MUSEUM

The creators of this good-size facility seem to have thought very carefully about what amuses kids most, and they were most definitely on the mark.

Pretend play has been taken to the limit. A fire station has full firefighter regalia, a real engine (the back, anyway) complete with hoses, and even a small fire pole to slide down. Kids like to see if they can place the boots just right so they can slide down the pole into them.

Little postal workers can sort and cancel mail behind the post-office counter and then take the bag and make deliveries around the room. Expect to be recruited as a customer in the grocery store, modeled after a large California chain. Thanks to a meat counter, lots of "food," and a working cash register with "money," it's about as close to the real thing as you can get without having the milk spoil.

## HEY, KIDS!
You've probably seen an ant farm; now find out what it feels like to live in one. InterAntics, the museum's newest attraction, is a 16-foot climbing sculpture in the form of a human-size ant farm. See if you can make it all the way to the top.

**KEEP IN MIND** Special events abound: Weekend workshops have featured cooking classes and mariachi dancing, and young children like the Caterpillar Club, Tuesday–Thursday afternoons. Seasonal events include October's Big Haunted House, with in-house trick-or-treating. The Rosebud Parade (November) lets kids take part in a mini version of the famed Rose Parade, complete with the Rose Queen and Court. Also look for the Eco-Arts Festival, culminating on Earth Day (April), and the Critter Expo, a display of creepy crawlies such as reptiles and bugs, in early summer.

 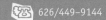

390 S. El Molino Ave., 2 blocks east of Lake Ave., Pasadena

626/449-9144

$5 ages 3 and up, $2.50 children 1–2, last M night of mth free

July–Aug, Su–Th 1–5, F–Sa 10–5; Sept–June, T 1:30–5, W–F and Su 1–5, Sa 10–5; last M of mth 5–8

2–10

Aspiring news anchors can do weather, sports, and news at the KCBS desk and then watch themselves on the monitor. And a full-size stage comes with dress-up clothes. Longing for the coast? The indoor "beach," one of the most popular spots in Kidspace, has many of the pleasures of the real thing, including sand, toys, and a cool breeze, courtesy of cranked-up air-conditioning.

Additional Kidspace activities include a small crafts area and the Mouse House, where computer lovers can try out some of the latest software. But not all exhibits here are inanimate. Critter Caverns is a mini zoo with reptiles and spiders. For those who want to get real close (be warned though; we're talking snakes and tarantulas here), museum staff are often on hand to bring out the creepy crawlers for personal inspection. The Caverns also includes a kid-size climbing area designed to re-create some of the animals' natural habitats. So if your children don't want to be with them, they can just be like them.

**KID-FRIENDLY EATS** Old Pasadena, the city's refurbished historic retail district, is full of places to eat, including the **Crocodile Cafe** (88 W. Colorado Blvd., tel. 626/568–9310), which features grills, pastas, and pizzas. Outside of Old Pasadena, in the Lake Avenue retail district, look for **Tony Roma's** (246 S. Lake Ave., tel. 626/405–0612), the well-known chain that serves up tasty ribs and other barbecue favorites.

# KNOTT'S BERRY FARM

While out-of-towners flock to the area's nationally known amusement behemoths, locals have come to cherish this home-grown favorite. Among southern Californians, Knott's is *the* place for rides: big ones, little ones, and just about everything in between.

Founded in the early 20th century as a berry farm (hence the name), this second-largest California amusement park might as well be called the not-so-little theme park that could. Its six theme areas—Ghost Town, Camp Snoopy, Siesta Village, Indian Trails, Wild Water Wildnerness, and the newest, the Boardwalk—comprise more than 165 rides, stage shows, and other attractions. Knott's youngest visitors feel at home in Camp Snoopy, where the Peanuts gang hangs out, and where little rides correspond to little people. There are mini trucks and scaled-down roller coasters, not to mention a bounce house, petting zoo, and miniature steam train. There's also an inventor's workshop, named for a guy called Edison, where you and your kids can tinker with a bunch of gadgets while learning basic science principles.

**HEY, KIDS!** The graveyard over in Ghost Town's Boot Hill boasts headstones from ghost towns throughout the western United States. Legend has it that one of the occupants still has a beating heart. Find it, says the legend—hint, you'll have to step on all the graves to locate the right one—and you'll always have good luck. You can use some of that good fortune when you search for treasure over at the Pan for Gold area of the town.

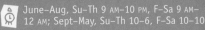
Lest you think the whole park is just for wee folk, Knott's also boasts a renowned collection of frighteningly fun coasters and other rides, including Boomerang (a definite local favorite), Jaguar!, Montezooma's Revenge, and HammerHead. You can just imagine what they're like. Among the newest additions are Supreme Scream, with three seconds of weightlessness while you shoot down 30 stories, and GhostRider, a wooden coaster rated one of the world's best by enthusiasts. In summer 2000, look for the Perilous Plunge water-drop ride—at 115 feet with a 75° decline. There are also plenty of equilibrium-annihilating rides with such fitting names as HeadSpin (migraine sufferers will be happy to know that HeadAche has been retired). Beyond those rides made to terrify or nauseate, novel creations include the charming Mystery Lodge, based on Native American stories, and Kingdom of the Dinosaurs, a dark ride back in time. If it's a blistering day, head to BigFoot Rapids, where the white water will more than likely leave you, shall we say, refreshed.

**KID-FRIENDLY EATS** Vendors sell meals, snacks, jams, and even boysenberry punch (Knott's invented the boysenberry). The main sit-down restaurant, **Mrs. Knott's Chicken Dinner Restaurant** (tel. 714/220–5080) is outside the gate (you'll need a hand stamp to return). Next door at **Chicken to Go,** you can get picnic fixings, and eat at any of Knott's tables and benches.

**KEEP IN MIND** Knott's can easily keep your family busy for a full day; if you've got little ones, you might never even make it out of Camp Snoopy. If you think you'll want to return to see more of the park or just to do it all again, ask about season passes for residents. The busiest days are in summer, but you can expect to wait on a few extra lines during special events, such as April's Easter EggMazement, the park's annual Easter Celebration, featuring the Easter Beagle. Still, though it does get busy, locals laud this park for being dependably less crowded than some of the better-known guys.

# LA BREA TAR PITS AND THE PAGE MUSEUM

Thousands of years ago, the Los Angeles basin was crowded with mammoths, bison, dire wolves, camels, and enormous 1-ton sloths. The bad news for them is that many wound up stuck in the black gunk that oozes from the La Brea Tar Pits. The good news for us is that their remains have been preserved in fossils that continue to be excavated from the site.

One of the richest sources of Ice Age fossils in the world, La Brea seems to yield an unending supply of immortalized remains. Literally millions of fossils have been recovered since the first documented find in about the mid-1700s, and the discoveries keep on coming. Though you can visit the tar pits year-round, they're idle 10 months a year. During July and August, however, you can watch the annual excavations in Pit 91 from special observation areas set up by the Page Museum, next door. (When strolling near the pits, wear good shoes and walk carefully, as the asphalt tends to ooze up all around.) The finds are pretty amazing, and fossilized bones in the dormant asphalt are sometimes visible to the naked eye.

## HEY, KIDS!

In Spanish, *brea* means "tar," so the translation of La Brea Tar Pits is actually the Tar Tar Pits. Though it's a bit repetitive, it certainly underscores the importance of that tar. Find out the strength of this gunk at the interactive Tar Vat, where you can try to manipulate a plunger stuck in goo.

## KEEP IN MIND

One note to visitors coming to ogle the site's dinosaur remains: There aren't any. Though dinosaurs are commonly associated with a landscape of bubbling ooze, no remains have ever been excavated here, since the pits date back only to the Ice Age (40,000 years ago) as opposed to the dinosaur age (65 million years ago). With membership, you get unlimited admission to the Page, the Natural History Museum, the Petersen Automotive Museum (*see below*), and the William S. Hart Museum.

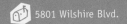 5801 Wilshire Blvd.

 Tar pits free; museum $6 ages 13 and up, $2 children 5–12

 Daily 10–5

 6 and up

323/934-7243

The bounty of all those finds can be seen at the museum, which is likely to excite most little kids, if only for the chance to see things from so many thousands of years ago. Displays include numerous painstakingly reconstructed fossilized skeletons as well as some millennium-old bones of the tar pits' only human victim ever retrieved. ("Was it an accident or Los Angeles's first murder victim?" asks the exhibit.) On one wall alone there are hundreds of dire wolf skulls, a tribute to just how many animals succumbed to the La Brea site. At the paleontology laboratory, in a nearby enclosure, your children can watch as fossils are cleaned up and preserved, providing a behind-the-scenes look at how all those fossilized clues to the past are pieced together.

**KID-FRIENDLY EATS** **Marie Callender's** (5773 Wilshire Blvd., tel. 323/937–7952), a stylish, upgraded link in the chain, contains a bit of vintage decor to accommodate the mid-Wilshire crowd while still offering a large, dependable menu. The **Farmer's Market** (633 W. 3rd St., tel. 323/954–4230) has a characteristically colorful atmosphere and numerous opportunities for alfresco dining. Among the vendors and restaurants here, you'll find everything from seafood to Mexican to deli.

# LEGOLAND

I f your single-digit-aged child feels shortchanged by some of the big-name theme parks that seem to cater to older, more adventurous tastes, this full-size theme park made for pint-size dispositions is bound to make a big splash. That's the draw of LEGOLAND. It's 128 acres of things to see and do, all designed expressly for the non-teen set.

About 1¼ hours south of Los Angeles, the park is worth the drive. Apart from its age designation, what sets it apart is its hands-on philosophy. Less a ride mecca than an interactive wonderland, LEGOLAND allows kids to be daring, putting them behind the wheels of boats and mini electric cars they can really drive. And since the cars aren't on tracks, you catch a glimpse of the future, watching as your children steer, accelerate and break (preferably not at the same time), obey traffic rules, and attend to road signs. Don't worry; they also have to wear a seatbelt. Other kid-motored adventures include the Sky Cycle, where kids pedal around an elevated track, and the Kid Power Tower, which requires passengers to work together to get to the top. But note well: The "reward" is a 35-foot "free fall" back down.

**HEY, KIDS!** Even if you're really little, you need not miss out on the experience of driving as LEGOLAND has a separate Junior Driving School, for kids age 3 to 5. Make sure to get to at least one of the shows. A favorite, at the Fun Town Stage, is the Big Test, in which Fun Town's Volunteer Fire Department performs acrobatics while teaching about fire safety. If you're lucky, you might even get a chance to join in.

In case you were wondering if there's actually any Lego here, get ready for the Lego art—30 million of those famous blocks fashioned into everything from giraffes and dragons to the White House and the Empire State Building. The Enchanted Walk and Safari both feature landmarks and animals made entirely out of Lego. Kids and adults alike have fun sightseeing in Miniland USA, whose many famous U.S. landmarks include the Washington Monument, the Manhattan skyline, and the Golden Gate Bridge. If all of that artwork inspires your youngsters, look for designated areas where they can experiment with Lego and Duplo creations of their own.

**KID-FRIENDLY EATS** The park's outdoor **Ristorante Brickolini** offers hand-tossed and wood-fired pizza and pastas made to order, while the **Knight's Table** can fill you up with barbecue favorites. LEGOLAND's sweet goodies, baked fresh on property, can be gotten at the **Fun Town Market** or the **Garden Restaurant and Bakery.**

**KEEP IN MIND** Opened in 1999, Carlsbad's LEGOLAND is only the third of its kind in the world (the other two are in Denmark and England). Since it's so new, expect crowds during peak times in summer and on holidays. Experiencing the whole park should take at least a full day, so plan on closing the park or coming back. Adults can accompany children on all rides except the Junior Driving Schools.

# LOS ANGELES COUNTY MUSEUM OF ART

You might think that this exceptional art museum should be your second choice now that the Getty Center has come to town. On the contrary, with more than 150,000 pieces in its permanent collection alone, the Los Angeles County Museum of Art (LACMA, as it's known to locals) has held on to its reputation as the most comprehensive U.S. art collection west of the Mississippi. It's also where you can find some of the more renowned traveling exhibits.

What this means for families is diversity, from Impressionists to Japanese art. Your kids will probably like the Anderson Building's second floor, with its colorful and sometimes playful collection of contemporary art. One example: a very large set of pool balls racked up and ready for play.

Spread across six buildings, LACMA covers a lot of territory. You can amble around the museum on your own or rent an audio tour. Unlike most recorded guides, this one allows you to wander in random order; just punch in the catalog number of the piece you're looking

KID-FRIENDLY EATS The museum's **Plaza Café** serves sandwiches, salads, and hot entrées. Or try the nearby **Marie Callender's** (see La Brea Tar Pits) or Beverly Hills' **Woo Lae Oak** (170 N. La Cienega Blvd., tel. 310/ 652–4187), where kids can cook food on hibachis at the table.

KEEP IN MIND Ask about the museum's exceptional extras, such as art, music, and film programs for both adults and children (extra fee required). If you find your kids enamored of the art scene, be sure to find time for another of the area's renowned institutions, the Norton Simon Museum (411 W. Colorado Blvd., Pasadena, tel. 626/449–6840). If you like what LACMA's Southwest Museum exhibit has to offer, try out the real thing (234 Museum Dr., tel. 323/221–2164), where you'll find a large collection of artifacts detailing the history and culture of the region's Native Americans.

5905 Wilshire Blvd., at Fairfax Ave.

 $7 adults, $1 children 5–18

 323/857–6000

M–T and Th 12–8, F 12–9, Sa–Su 11–8

All ages

at and listen. Only a fraction of the museum's pieces are included on the tour, however, which can be frustrating. Still, it's a great gimmick for families, particularly since some narration is tagged specially for kids.

The tour is just one way the museum has become increasingly child friendly of late. Other innovations include the new Experimental Gallery (in the LACMA West building), which has 10,000 square feet of exhibit space geared for kids. Much of what's here is interactive, including video stations, CD-ROM computers, and Discovery Boxes with age-appropriate activities. Exhibits rotate about every nine months, roughly with the school year. Also in LACMA West, look for satellite exhibits of the Southwest Museum, a separate and unrelated facility (and the city's oldest museum) whose main location isn't large enough to house its entire collection. The LACMA space, a colorful adobe-like facility designed by Disney Imagineers, features some of the Southwest Museum's comprehensive collection of southwest American art. But rest assured; the art here is definitely not Mickey Mouse.

**HEY, KIDS!** Don't miss the walk-through garage on the Anderson Building's second floor. Entitled *Central Meridian, 1981*, it's a fascinating artistic tribute to that all-American storage facility. Everything is authentic, down to the musty smell. The collection includes snowshoes, trophies, a moose head, a broken TV, and a chalkboard with a scientific formula. How many things are in your garage? Note the car: It had to be sawed in half and rejoined to get it in.

# LOS ANGELES ZOO

When they want to visit animals, many Angelenos head a couple of hours down the 405 to the San Diego Zoo. But this nice-size zoo, in the heart of Griffith Park, has a lot to like, especially since it's been shined up recently. For a pleasant and relatively cost-conscious family afternoon, you'd do well to stay local and visit this Los Angeles animal kingdom.

Wend your way through natural habitats in the zoo's five distinct "continents:" Africa, Australia, Eurasia, North America, and South America. Overall, there are about 1,200 animals here, all displayed in an up-close fashion that allows you to fully appreciate their height (giraffes) and girth (elephants).

The Chimpanzees of the Mahale Mountains, the first new exhibit in nearly a decade, marks a rebirth for the zoo. With reasonably natural habitats on either side of a pane of glass, two species of primate get an unusual—pretty much nose-to-nose—view of one another. Watching the chest-pounding humans and seemingly bemused chimps, it's hard to tell who's performing for whom. Still, there's no question that it's a happy close encounter between not-so-distant relatives. Kids

KEEP IN MIND Though decidedly smaller than the San Diego Zoo, there's still plenty of territory to cover—80 acres—so be sure to put on your walking shoes. If you'd prefer a little help with the long haul, get a daily shuttle pass, which entitles you to hop on and off the shuttle to different areas of the zoo. If it's a scorchingly hot day, go hang out with the koalas in their indoor habitat. The air-conditioned exhibit makes a prime respite for humans as well, and besides, these cute creatures do wonders for any midafternoon grumpiness.

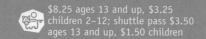

particularly love when the baby chimps exhibit habits their own parents would reprimand them for. Look for the arrival of an orangutan exhibit—the second part of what will ultimately become the zoo's great-ape forest—some time in the year 2000.

In addition to the main exhibits, the facility has a children's zoo, called Adventure Island, that features the Animals and You show as well as a baby-animal nursery. A petting zoo is expected in the future.

Special exhibitions, such as the World of Birds show, are held during the day, so check your map for a show schedule upon arrival. The zoo is also known for some truly special events, such as its Boo in the Zoo weekend right before Halloween, when kids can go trick-or-treating throughout the grounds. It may not have real ghosts and goblins, but it sure has a *big* black cat (a black jaguar).

**KID-FRIENDLY EATS** There are several places to eat right inside the zoo, including **Adventure Island Grill,** for burgers, hot dogs, and sandwiches, and **Silverback's Cafe,** for pizza, salads, and Italian sandwiches. Outside the park, **Island's** (*see* Griffith Park Horse Rental) offers a taste of the tropics alongside more traditional fare.

**HEY, KIDS!** When you're up at the glass at the chimpanzee exhibit, put your hand on the glass; sometimes the chimpanzees will match their hand to yours. Which one is bigger? Also, look for animal prints in Adventure Island. Then step on them and listen for the corresponding animal sounds. Can you guess whose footprints you're following?

# MARINA PARK

Lovers of sand and surf have long dubbed southern California's beaches *the* places to be. These, after all, are the beaches of lore, immortalized in song and on screen by the Beach Boys, *Baywatch,* and *Beverly Hills, 90210*. But contrary to popular belief, not all of southern California's coastline is frequented by tanned bodies in bikinis and boxers sporting headphones and multiple body piercings and rollerblading up and down the boardwalk. (For that, *see* Venice Beach.) Some area beaches are actually downright congenial.

If you're looking for the truly tame (in the water and out), you can't beat Marina Park. Located on a quiet stretch past the Alamitos Bay Marina, this is a so-called "Mother's Beach"—characterized by a calm, toddler-friendly current that attracts lots of families. It's the antithesis of the 6-foot-swell-laden beaches that have made California a surfer's heaven; in fact, there are no waves to speak of. (Even Long Beach's ocean waves stay on the small side, thanks to a manmade breakwater built several miles off the coast.) The smallish bay beach—one regular quips that how big it feels depends on how many kids you have with

**KEEP IN MIND** Another Mother's Beach is Marina Beach (Admiralty Way and Via Marina, Marina Del Rey, tel. 310/305–9545). Older kids like the vast sand and activities at Will Rogers State Beach (14800 Pacific Coast Hwy., Pacific Palisades, tel. 310/394–3264). For surfing, check out Huntington State Beach (21601 Pacific Coast Hwy., at Magnolia Blvd., Huntington Beach, tel. 714/536–1454), home to the International Surfing Museum (411 Olive Ave., Huntington Beach, tel. 714/960–3483), the only place, according to the ad, where it's "OK to call the curator 'Dude.' "

5839 Appian Way, off 2nd St., Long Beach

 Daily 8–sunset

 562/570-3215

 Free

All ages

you—is the place for young children to safely splash in the surf or to build sand castles without fear of being swept away by the undertow. Though water gets deeper as you go further out, buoys clearly mark the shallow area, and the drop-off is gradual rather than a sudden plunge. Best of all, watercraft passing outside the designated swimming area are slowed to a mere 5 miles per hour, and speeds are strictly enforced. And, though you must keep watch over your own children, it's nice to know that lifeguards are on duty.

In addition to the de rigeur stretches of sand and water, the park has a playground and a picnic area. If you'd like to use the site for a birthday party (a popular prospect), call the coordinator (tel. 562/570-3215) to make arrangements. Also note that though the beach is free, parking isn't.

**KID-FRIENDLY EATS** Refreshments are available from the picnic area's vendor, or you can bring you own. If you'd rather let someone else cook, try the big American menu at **Hof's Hut** (4828 E. 2nd St., tel. 562/439–4775), offering sandwiches, hamburgers, and other traditional family fare. Little ones willing to go beyond PB&Js and chicken nuggets can venture with you to any of numerous Belmont Shores area eateries, including **Super Mex** (4711 E. 2nd St., tel. 562/439–4489), serving fast, good Mexican food.

# MISSION SAN JUAN CAPISTRANO

Most people know this southern California mission for its annual ornithological phenomena (the famed swallows make their entrance and exit on March 19 and October 23, respectively) and the resultant 1930s tune "When the Swallows Come Back to Capistrano," which the gift-shop clerk might happily sing for you, if you ask. These days, however, you're more likely to see pigeons here than swallows. Some say that noisy restoration work has sent them away, but staff here assert that swallows have simply followed the human migration to the suburbs (you'll find lots of nests on surrounding homes—much to some residents' chagrin). But the 200-year-old Mission San Juan Capistrano—the so-called "jewel" of California's 21 Spanish missions—is a worthy historic adventure nonetheless. Built in 1776, the vast and majestic site feels as grand as an ancient European castle, an enchanting place to soak up some history with your kids while you explore its spacious rooms, botanical gardens, and ruins.

**KEEP IN MIND** Festivals and special events at the mission take full advantage of the lovely surroundings. Saturday evenings from June through October, bring a picnic supper and enjoy the outdoor concerts, which start at about 6:30. In February, the Lincoln Festival celebrates the former president's important role in the mission's history (he signed the document that returned the missions to the Catholic church) with food, activities, and a visit by Mr. Lincoln himself. And of course, the Swallows Festival (March 19), celebrating the return of the famed birds to the area, if not just the mission.

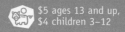

You're first struck by the ruins of the Great Stone Church, one of the elements that lends the place the feel of another era. History is so well preserved here, in fact, that it's a shock to see the taco stand sign sticking up over the outside wall. Strolling around, it's easy to imagine life here a couple of centuries ago. Some of the more interesting spots include the old Soldier's Barracks, built to house the few military men that were stationed here long ago; the mission cemetery; the Serra Chapel; and the small museum depicting life at the mission. In the ethereal Sacred Garden, 18th-century bells hang in graceful archways.

Although you can visit any time, the best way to get a feel for the place is to come on a Living History Day, held once a month. On those days, volunteers appear in colorful period attire; adopt the character of Spanish soldiers, Juaneño Indians, and other former mission residents; and interact with visitors.

**KID-FRIENDLY EATS** The mission sits inside a particularly cute town with many places to eat. You can dine in at or take out from the **Diedrich Cafe** (31760 Camino Capistrano, tel. 949/488– 2150). Why not pick up some soup, salad, or a sandwich and have a picnic in the mission? Nearby, there's also a **Ruby's** (31781 Camino Capistrano, tel. 949/496–7829).

**HEY, KIDS!** Look for bird-food dispensers spread around the mission. A handful of feed costs 25¢; if you're brave (and fortunate), birds will come and eat directly out of your hands. Over the years, these well-fed birds (feathered friends here, are, shall we say, on the stout side) have become accustomed to their two-legged friends. Birds will land on your shoulder and in your hair. But beware: They're not potty trained.

# MOVIELAND WAX MUSEUM

The future of today's celebrities may not be carved in stone, but they're at least preserved in wax at this museum. Offbeat but well done, the enterprise is one of a couple of wax museums in Los Angeles (*see* the Hollywood Entertainment Museum entry for information about another) that have become a staple of the true southern California tourist experience. Included are incarnations of many past and present luminaries, from Michael Jackson (replete in his original "Bad" video ensemble) to John Wayne, Dorothy to President Clinton. Though some may call it hokey (and it is a little), it does make for a fun afternoon. And there is something marvelously intriguing about just how real these wax folks can seem.

All the exhibits have themes, many featuring accompanying soundtracks with music and dialogue. Among the most elaborate ensembles are the original *Star Trek* crew standing in a replica of the Starship *Enterprise*'s bridge and a scene from the depths of the doomed ship in the *Poseidon Adventure,* featuring Gene Hackman, Ernest Borgnine, Stella Stevens, and a lot of running water. Some of the figurines here are amazingly lifelike: Dick Martin,

## HEY, KIDS!

Don't forget to look for tidbits of trivia scattered about the exhibits. For instance, bet you didn't know that *Rowan and Martin's Laugh-In* started the "knock, knock" joke craze or that Michael Jackson, in typically eccentric fashion, helped dress his own likeness during a midnight, post-concert visit here.

## KEEP IN MIND

A leisurely stroll through the museum will take a couple of hours. If you're feeling energetic, pair Movieland with the Ripley's Believe It or Not! Museum (*see below*), across the street. A combined ticket to the two museums will actually net you a discount; you'll have to use half the day you buy it, but the other ticket is good indefinitely. The busiest times at this museum are during school breaks, but even a summer visit can be surprisingly crowd-free and can make for a nice air-conditioned interlude to boot.

7711 Beach Blvd., off Rte. 91, Buena Park

 $12.95 ages 12 and up,
$6.95 children 4–11

 M–F 10–6, Sa–Su 9–7

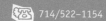 714/522–1154

All ages

one half of the Rowan and Martin comedy team, and Bette Davis, to name two. Others are, shall we say, less than true to their originals, but dissing is half the fun.

A collection of chillingly convincing figures can be found in the Chamber of Horrors, where Jason of *Friday the 13th* fame looks real enough to raise neck hairs. You might also back away from the mummy, who seems poised to sit up. Not everyone will be enamored of the creepy critters, and some kids may be downright terrified of them. Fortunately, you can skirt the dungeon theme altogether by following the arrows. Alas, the detour leads you into another house of horrors, a vast bulk candy shop. In fact, shops are interspersed throughout the Movieland experience, including one where you can insert your face into famous movie posters, such as those for *Gone with the Wind* and the *Wizard of Oz*.

Be sure to stop on the way out to check out the photo with George Burns you posed for on the way in. There's an extra charge for purchase, though.

**KID-FRIENDLY EATS** **PoFolks** (7701 Beach Blvd., tel. 714/521–8955), right next door, serves virtually every incarnation of chicken you and your kids can imagine. At **Claim Jumper** (7971 Beach Blvd., tel. 714/523–3227), families can ogle the wild-game heads on the wall while eating hearty portions of pork ribs, hamburgers, fish, and steaks. Also *see* dining entries in Ripley's Believe It or Not! Museum.

# MUSEUM OF FLYING

In the annals of childhood imagination, playing pilot ranks right up there with being a firefighter or a western cowpoke. So it stands to reason that the Museum of Flying is a mighty popular place among families. Fortunately, it takes its role as educator and entertainer to, well, new heights. A diverse collection of things you can get into, steer, and experiment with, the museum is one of those places families like to come back to over and over, if only to master some of its gadgets.

Located in a Santa Monica Airport hangar, the museum is immediately striking for its display of colorful World War II–era planes (originals and replicas) suspended overhead and parked on the ground. War veterans and kids alike seem captivated by these aluminum and steel legends, most of them still in working order, including such biplanes as the *Yellow Relic* Navy plane and the bright orange 1932 WACO. Of particular pride to the museum is the *New Orleans,* one of the first planes to fly around the world. (Its companion plane is displayed at the Smithsonian's National Air and Space Museum.) Active runways just beyond the open hangar

**HEY, KIDS!** If you're in the mood for action, look for flight-theme arcade games as well as the vintage Armed Service Gunnery Trainer, essentially the equivalent of an old-style video game. A stationary simulator will give you the experience of sitting inside a cockpit, but if you're roughly 5 to 10 years old, you can pilot a moving flight simulator. Using joysticks and pedals, you can operate the flaps and rudder and cause the plane to bank left and right.

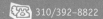 2772 Donald Douglas Loop N, north side of
Santa Monica Airport, Santa Monica

 310/392-8822

 $7 adults, $3
children 3–17

 W–Su 10–5

All ages

door provide for perfect views of takeoffs and landings by small jets, helicopters, and even some of the museum's stock of restored antique aircraft, such as the Japanese Zero Warbird and a P-51 Mustang (both rare originals). Also outside is the shell of a Korean War–era helicopter (think *M\*A\*S\*H*) that your child can climb in and pretend to fly.

Inside the museum are plenty more interactive exhibits, including simulators, an activity about the science of flying, and another helicopter to sit in. This one even has some working parts, which can entertain imaginative children for some time. Upstairs, you can all get a better look at the suspended planes and use headphones to listen in on air-traffic controllers at both the Santa Monica and Los Angeles airports. Getting your kids back down to earth might not be so easy.

## KID-FRIENDLY EATS

In addition to serving up tasty California cuisine, **DC-3** (2800 Donald Douglas Loop N, tel. 310/399–2323) offers a supervised evening children's program; kids get fed and play at the museum while parents dine (reservations required). Colorful **Acapulco** (3360 Ocean Park Blvd., tel. 310/450–8665) serves Mexican and American food.

## KEEP IN MIND

Feel free to ask questions of the knowledgeable volunteer docents. Also inquire about the upstairs movie theater, which shows short subjects (roughly 15 minutes)—from documentaries to Blue Angels stunt films to an occasional Charlie Brown picture about the history of flight. As for the moving flight simulator, be warned that the sensation of motion thrills some kids and terrifies others, so prepare your children accordingly. If you're here on a quiet day, the docents are likely to allow a longer "flight."

# MUSEUM OF NEON ART

If you're having trouble convincing your kids to make a foray to an art museum, this colorful place may be just the place to start.

The only museum of its kind in the world, the Museum of Neon Art is dedicated to all kinds of electric art: kinetic, neon, and otherwise. At only 7,500 square feet, it's a relatively small space, with just enough oversize and brightly colored pieces to engage some of the smallest budding art enthusiasts.

Begun in the 1980s by an "electric" artist who wanted to exhibit her work, the museum houses its own permanent collection as well as a series of traveling exhibits, rotated several times during the year. Some of the pieces are pure nostalgia, such as the RCA Victor, Chief Motel, and Colonial Dairy signs; more of the museum's vintage neon-sign collection can be found at Universal Studios CityWalk, one of the few places that can accommodate such extra-large pieces. There's also some icon art, such as a 12-foot by 12-foot Elvis.

**HEY, KIDS!** In a regular light bulb, light is produced by passing electricity through a tiny piece of metal, which then glows hot. But in a neon light, it's actually a type of gas that glows when electrified. Strictly speaking, neon is only one of those gases, the kind that produces a bright reddish-orange color. Argon, for example, glows greenish blue. But because neon became the most commonly used gas in advertising signs, the name "neon" stuck for all such gas-filled lights.

 501 W. Olympic Blvd.

 213/489-9918

 $5 adults, $3.50 students 13–22, 2nd Th of mth 5–8 free

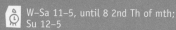 W–Sa 11–5, until 8 2nd Th of mth; Su 12–5

10 and up

Many pieces, however, fall into a more intangible category. The Plasma Ball—one of the museum's few interactive exhibits—allows you to press a button to unleash a bolt of current and watch it shoot through a glass ball.

Staff at this unique facility are loathe to categorize its wares as strictly pop art. Though pop pieces are definitely here, the museum regards neon as more of a tool than a style, with the lights considered the coloring equivalent of paint. Interestingly, according to those who work here, children are often more open to the exhibits than their parents, who are occasionally reticent to categorize neon as a true art form.

**KID-FRIENDLY EATS** The greasy-spoon fare at the **Original Pantry Cafe** (877 S. Figueroa St., tel. 213/972–9279) has made this 24-hour restaurant owned by L.A.'s mayor a city institution. The cheap diner food includes some pretty good steaks, and the atmosphere is bustling. For dependable Italian fare, try **La Bella Cucina** (949 S. Figueroa St., tel. 213/623–0014).

# MUSEUM OF TOLERANCE

The metal detector and bag search at the door is a not-so-subtle reminder of the sensitive issues tackled by this groundbreaking institution. Opened in 1993, this museum isn't a typical entertainment stop on the Hollywood tour, but it's a must-see nonetheless. Educational, fascinating, and occasionally gut-wrenching, the museum explores racism, bigotry, and the Holocaust in a package that's sure to engender conversation around your dinner table.

Though the museum dwells considerably on the Holocaust, it devotes equal time to present-day racism and bigotry. Hands-on activities in the Tolerancenter allow you and your family to explore human-rights violations both abroad (the former Yugoslavia) and at home (the American civil rights movement). More strikingly, though, it encourages kids to consider their own prejudices and stereotypes. The Manipulator, a videotaped man who greets you by voicing extreme prejudices, is disarmingly effective at this. Many displays are innovative and complex, but the lower-tech variety—such as a simple map highlighting more than 250 U.S. hate groups—can speak volumes, too.

**HEY, KIDS!** For a unique experience, visit the Point of View Diner. You can't eat here, but you can take stock of your views from a "menu" of personal-responsibility subjects—from drunk driving to hate speech—and compare them with other visitors around you. The differences in opinion may surprise you. In case you're wondering just how effective the Museum of Tolerance is, California law enforcers are required to visit here as part of their rookie training.

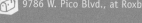 9786 W. Pico Blvd., at Roxbury Dr.

 $8.50 ages 11 and up, $5.50 students, $3.50 children 3–10

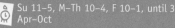 Su 11–5, M–Th 10–4, F 10–1, until 3 Apr–Oct

310/553–8403

 11 and up

Part two of the experience, the dramatic and effective Holocaust section, explores World War II Germany by taking you back to witness events leading up to the war. This section can be disarming and chilling, particularly the macabre recorded reenactment of the famed Wannsee Conference, during which Nazi officers casually discuss the "Final Solution" and the best method for disposing of their victims.

Overall, the museum's strength is how it humanizes its subjects. Through dramatic film montages, many created by Oscar-winning filmmakers, formerly faceless Bosnian, Jewish, and American civil rights movement victims—and even the perpetrators—become individuals. Such humanization reaches a pinnacle in the Holocaust section, where Passport Cards, drawn by visitors at the outset of the exhibit, document the travails of various European children affected by the war; a computer printout at the end reveals the fate of the child you picked.

## KID-FRIENDLY EATS

**Bob Morris's Beverly Hills BBQ** (9740 W. Pico Blvd., tel. 310/553–5513) serves tasty barbecue right next door to the museum. Ribs, chicken, and pulled-pork sandwiches all leave you licking your fingers. **Factor's Famous Deli** (9420 W. Pico Blvd., tel. 310/278–9175) dishes up super-size delicatessen sandwiches stuffed with salami, pastrami, and more.

## KEEP IN MIND

During the school year, avoid mornings, which are often sold out with school groups. Beware of the dramatic film clips, some of which contain stark images—too graphic for children under 11. The museum, however, does offer monthly storytelling programs and other activities aimed at the younger set; call for details. The Museum of Tolerance features daily speakers, including occasional visits by a former neo-Nazi skinhead, as well as thrice-daily (weekdays at 1, 2, and 3; check for Sunday schedule) talks by Holocaust survivors.

# NATURAL HISTORY MUSEUM

People are often surprised to learn that the city best known for movie stars and glamour also has one of the largest natural history museums in the country. Number three behind the Smithsonian's National Museum of Natural History, in Washington, and New York's American Museum of Natural History, Los Angeles's Natural History Museum captivates kids with examples of nature from prehistoric to modern, including dinosaur bones, shark skeletons, and live insects.

You're greeted outside by bronze casts of a couple of dueling dinos. Inside are the real things—well, real bones anyway. Huge reconstructed beasts—a T-Rex and a triceratops posed in combat—prompt jaw-dropped stares, and occasionally some frightened whimpers, from kids astonished by the fabled creatures' actual size.

There are more remains all along the Dinosaur Hall on the way to the Discovery Center, where your kids can touch a dinosaur skeleton, dig for fossils in a sand pit, and make

## HEY, KIDS!
Look for educators in the Insect Zoo. They can answer questions and may even let you touch some specimens. And don't forget to open the zoo's refrigerator to find out what all those bugs really eat (hold on to your lunch when examining the meal of the dung beetle).

## KEEP IN MIND
Annual membership at the Natural History Museum is a particular bargain, because it also covers unlimited admission to the Page Museum (*see* the La Brea Tar Pits), the Petersen Automotive Museum (*see below*), and the William S. Hart Museum (24151 San Fernando Rd., Newhall, tel. 661/254–4584), a mansion and ranch that once belonged to the former Western film star. In addition, you'll get mailings detailing an unbelievable collection of family overnights and adventures. Check out the museum each May, when it holds the annual Insect Fair, the largest event of its kind.

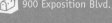

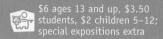

crayon rubbings from a fossil rock. Little kids often flock to a collection of taxidermic animals they can actually touch. The lion—dog-eared from many years of being loved—seems to be a particular toddler favorite. Older kids can engage in tasks set forward in activity boxes. Resident live animals include a 12-foot (caged!) python and a huge Pacu fish, a 4-foot swimmer that 3-foot children are happy to discover is a devout vegetarian.

Once you've torn your children away from the Discovery Center (a major feat for most kids), you can head to another favorite: the Insect Zoo, home to such crawly critters as tarantulas, cockroaches, stick bugs, millipedes, and centipedes. Though moms and dads may cringe, the "ick" factor seems to be lost on kids, who have been known to spend many hours getting to know their eight-, 10- and 100-legged friends. Other hot spots in the museum include the Gem Vault, containing rubies, diamonds, etc., as well as the marine and bird halls.

KID-FRIENDLY EATS The museum itself has the **Curator's Cafe,** a cafeteria-style restaurant with salads, hot dogs, and macaroni and cheese as well as special items of the day. On Figueroa, look for **Margarita Jones** (3760 S. Figueroa St., tel. 213/747-4400), a Mexican restaurant that features food for adult and kids' tastes. Ask about the specialty of the house, the *carne asada* (broiled beef).

# OLVERA STREET

Most people think of the heart of Los Angeles as Hollywood, but the City of Angels has its roots here, on and around Olvera Street, a place that's been brimming with life since long before the first movie director yelled, "Action."

Settled in 1781 by 11 Mexican families, the Olvera Street historic district heralds its heritage in particularly colorful style. The retail area (created as a tourist attraction in 1930) mimics the charm of a traditional Mexican marketplace, with numerous shops and vendor stands selling everything from clothing and hats to piñatas and hand-crafted pottery. Visit on weekends and you may also happen upon mariachis and folkloric dance troupes. Of course, half the fun of coming here is eating, and there's plenty of that, too. In addition to a few sit-down restaurants, there are numerous homespun proprietors pedaling authentic Mexican fare—the real heartburn-inducing versions!—including burritos, tacos, and taquitos.

**HEY, KIDS!** Throughout the year, the community celebrates traditional and colorful Mexican festivals and holidays. In April, let Fido be the center of attention at the Blessing of the Animals. On this day, people bring in their pets—anything from the family dog to a pet pig to your favorite snake—to be blessed by the Catholic Church. The day-long event, an ancient Spanish tradition, is held on the Old Plaza and starts with a parade and the traditional blessing rite.

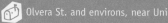

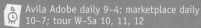

On both sides of the marketplace are historic buildings. You can get to know them either on your own or on a free 60-minute guided walking tour. Either way, you'll want to hit a few significant stops, most notably the Avila Adobe (10 E. Olvera St.). Built in 1818, this oldest home in Los Angeles is frozen in time, with everything as it was nearly 200 years ago. The Sepulveda House Museum (622 N. Main St.) is an old Eastlake Victorian boardinghouse containing exhibits and showing an 18-minute video on the history of Los Angeles, and the old Plaza Firehouse Museum (134 Paseo de la Plaza) is the city's oldest firehouse. The Old Plaza (1825), formerly the town square, features statues and plaques paying homage to the area's founders and hosts occasional music and dance concerts, with performances ranging from folklore to Latin rock. Our Lady Queen of Angels (535 N. Main St.), also known as the Old Plaza Church, dates back to 1818 and is the oldest in L.A. Still an active Catholic parish, the church is open daily for on-your-own tours.

**KEEP IN MIND** It's a good idea to call ahead before venturing here, as tourist attractions and restaurants often adjust their hours. For more insight into Los Angeles's cultural heritage, be sure to visit some of the city's other ethnic neighborhoods, including Chinatown and Little Tokyo, the latter of which features the Japanese American National Museum (369 E. 1st St., tel. 213/625–0414).

**KID-FRIENDLY EATS** There are lots of restaurants to choose from all along Olvera Street. **La Golondrina** (17 W. Olvera St., tel. 213/628–4349), one of the area's largest eateries, features specialty Mexican entrées, such as *mole poblano* (chicken with chilis and nuts and chocolate sauce) and traditional Mexican fajitas. People go to **El Paseo** (11 E. Olvera St., tel. 213/626–1361) for the fresh, handmade tortillas and guacamole, as well as enchiladas, tostadas, and other entrées. Both offer indoor and outdoor seating.

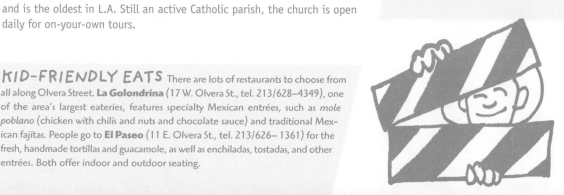

# ORANGE COUNTY MARINE INSTITUTE

One family calls Dana Point Harbor the home of the pirate ship. The two-masted vessel in question is actually an exact replica of the brig *Pilgrim,* the 19th-century ship famous for carrying Richard Henry Dana, Jr., (author of *Two Years before the Mast*) on his perilous journey from Boston to California. (The word "brig" refers not to the *Pilgrim*'s jail but to its rigging—the configuration of sails—during the mid-1800s.) The fantasy-inspiring tall ship, owned by the Orange County Marine Institute, opens its gangway to tourists most Sundays, allowing kids to explore the ship's many nooks and crannies as well as to visit with its crew of sailors, decked out in 1830s period attire.

But there's more to the institute than the period sea vessel. Like Dana himself, your family can become explorers, tagging along with the institute's staff of marine biologists as they study the ocean on a state-of-the-art research vessel, the R/V *Sea Explorer.* While on these 1½- and 2½-hour educational cruises (including some on weekend evenings), you'll see not only sea lions and other playful creatures, but also lesser-known inhabitants of the

## HEY, KIDS!

Yes, Dana Point was named for Dana, who romanticized the area in his writing. He took to the sea after he was caught cheating at Harvard. Later he completed law school, and his book is now a classic. The moral: Don't be discouraged by hard times (but don't cheat, either!).

**KEEP IN MIND** It's best to reserve spots on a cruise two to three weeks in advance, but last-minute reservations, even in season, are sometimes available. Be sure to bring your bikes. A 3-mile trail goes all the way from the harbor to Capo Beach; halfway there, at Doheny State Beach, you can rent a surrey, a pedal-powered cart. A sailing ship, a research boat, a bike, and a surrey sure make for a day of varied and interesting transportation.

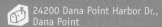

waters. Some of the most eye-popping finds, in fact, are uncovered when the trawl net comes up with creatures that live on the bottom. Biologists also throw out a plankton net—you'll get to look at what's caught under a microscope—as well as another that trawls for fish.

Half the fun of these cruises is that you never know what you might see. Though the boat runs year-round, you'll get a fringe benefit if you travel during the winter months (January–April). That's when the Pacific gray whales make their annual migration. An up-close look at one of these majestic creatures is truly awe-inspiring. Whatever you see, though, you can count on getting completely caught up in the experience. The amiable marine biologists seem to truly revel in sharing their work with young explorers and pepper the entire adventure with their infectious enthusiasm. Once back at port, be sure to stop by the institute's touch tanks (in the Lab and Whale Room), where you can handle resident sea creatures such as hermit crabs and sea stars.

**KID-FRIENDLY EATS** **John's Fish Market** (34665 Street of the Golden Lantern, tel. 949/496-2807) is known for fresh, inexpensive seafood enjoyed indoors or out. Apart from the food (burgers, sandwiches, salads), the calling card of **Proud Mary's** (34689 Street of the Golden Lantern, tel. 949/493-5853) is stellar coastal views. You can dine inside or out here, too. The **Brig** (34461 Street of the Golden Lantern, tel. 949/496-9046) serves burgers, seafood, sandwiches, and, on Mondays, all-you-can-eat ribs.

# PACIFIC PARK

If you're going to go to an amusement park, why not make it a park with scenery? That's what you'll get at Pacific Park, a charming seaside recreation area sitting right at the edge of the Pacific Ocean on the walkway of the Santa Monica Pier. It has that throwback feel of old-time amusement areas, with rides, restaurants, and junk food, not to mention classic carnival-style games where you can throw basketballs or spray squirt guns to win gloriously homely stuffed animals.

Pacific Park is a descendant of the old Looff Pleasure Pier, which closed in the 1940s. (The Looff Carousel at the entrance to the pier is actually a vestige of the original.) In 1996, an infusion of cash brought the place back to its original splendor, and more recently, the boardwalk atmosphere has been plumped up by the continuing flow of new attractions designed to appeal to the more adventurous, as well as the pint-size, amusement park enthusiast.

**HEY, KIDS:** Once you're done above the pier, ask your parents if you can check out what's below at the UCLA Ocean Discovery Center. Here a collection of touch tanks lets you get up close and personal with sea life from the Santa Monica Bay, including starfish, sea urchins, and hermit crabs. Large tanks house bigger creatures, such as shark and octopus. Don't miss the chance to watch the sharks eat their squid meals; ask about feeding times on the way in.

Santa Monica Pier, western end of
Colorado Ave., Santa Monica

 Free, attractions
$1.25–$4 each, Ocean
Discovery Center $3

 Mem. Day–Labor Day, Su–Th 10 AM–11 PM,
F–Sa 10 AM–12 AM; early Sept–late May, M–Th
11–6, F 11 AM–12 AM, Sa 10 AM–12 AM, Su 10–9

310/260–8744, 310/393–6149
Ocean Discovery Center

2 and up

Stalwarts among Pacific's 12 rides include the 130-foot-tall Ferris Wheel, from which you can all but see forever (those afraid of heights need not apply). A 55-foot-high roller coaster offers additional views, but at only 35 mph, don't expect super thrills. Bumper cars include a version for adults and a mini one, creatively named PCH Driving School, expressly for kids. Modern additions include two flight simulators, both of which rank as some of the park's more expensive rides. Simulator programs change periodically, so check what adventure is departing during your visit. You may get sent on an undersea adventure (the Bottlenose) or on a more exciting journey through an active volcano. Be sure to look out for some of the park's live entertainment, and don't forget to bring the bikes and blades; just off the pier lies some of the best paved beach-side trails for wheeling and rolling along.

KID-FRIENDLY EATS Along the pier, you'll find everything from hot dogs to chicken to seafood. A short walk away, the burgers at **Johnny Rockets** (1322 3rd St., tel. 310/394–6362) are always hits with kids. Also within walking distance, the **Crocodile Café** (101 Santa Monica Blvd., tel. 310/394–4783) serves up crayons and color-in menus alongside a selection of American favorites.

KEEP IN MIND Pacific tends to change its hours seasonally. In addition, during off-season (roughly the day after Labor Day to the day before Memorial Day), Pacific Park offers limited operations, meaning only a few rides and games are open (the Ferris wheel, however, always runs). Call ahead for specific times and attractions. Finally, while the pier is definitely a nice place to spend an afternoon, expect those ride prices to add up. If you forgot the skates and cycles, rent them at Sea Mist Rentals (1619 Ocean Front Walk, tel. 310/395–7076).

# PALACE PARK

Video games never looked like this when we parents were kids! (Remember Pong?) A virtual playground of the highest order, Palace Park—easily identifiable from I–405 as the building that looks like a castle—is the place for your kids to go to "buzz," "beep," and "whrrr" to their heart's delight.

At 11 acres, Palace Park is one of the largest family entertainment center/arcades in the area. The arcade section looks like a computer-age casino, with electronic boxes lined up row by row and kids and adults careening, steering, and shooting around virtual ski mountains, speedways, and shooting ranges. The cacophony of electronic sounds can be overwhelming, but once in front of the screen, it's hard to tear yourself or your children away. From jet skiing to playing football to dinosaur hunting, the games involve you completely. Races can be run solo or hooked up to challenge others. Each game dispenses tickets (commensurate with your score) that can be traded in for prizes at the on-site redemption center.

**KEEP IN MIND** Currently, games use one to four tokens, but that could increase as games become more sophisticated. In any case, you can go through a lot fast. (Using 12 tokens and getting 24 tickets in 15 minutes is typical.) Lest you think you'll get something wonderful for all that money, think again. Though some prizes cost five tickets, the big ones will probably cost more than you have. For example, an enormous stuffed bear requires a mere 11,000 tickets. Palace Entertainment (tel. 949/261–0404), Palace Park's owner, operates three other parks in the area; call for locations.

 3405 Michelson Dr., off I-405, Irvine

 949/559-8336

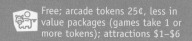 Free; arcade tokens 25¢, less in value packages (games take 1 or more tokens); attractions $1–$6

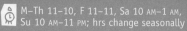 M–Th 11–10, F 11–11, Sa 10 AM–1 AM, Su 10 AM–11 PM; hrs change seasonally

 3 and up

Next door, laser tag enthusiasts can pursue their sport in particularly elaborate style. The 3,000-square-foot arena—lauded by many fans as the best of its kind—is replete with fog machines, not to mention plenty of places to duck and hide from the "enemy." Also indoors is a flight-simulator ride; outside, look for go-carts, bumper boats, batting cages, and miniature golf. The latest outdoor additions include a 32-foot-high rock-climbing wall and a skateboard park with a street course and half pipe. (If all that isn't enough, you can traipse next door and line 'em up for some old-fashioned entertainment—bowling—at Irvine Lanes.)

Though particularly popular among teenagers, Palace Park has taken care to ensure that the whole family can get involved. Most rides allow riders as small as 42" (there's even a miniature go-cart just for them), and there are plenty of scaled-down arcade games that little ones can play for prizes.

**KID-FRIENDLY EATS** There's a **McDonald's Express** (tel. 949/759–8517) right inside, serving the fast-food giant's standard fare. Just up the street in the Park Place Plaza complex, you can choose from scads of popular chain restaurants, including **Left at Albuquerque** (3309 Michelson Dr., tel. 949/757–7600). Its southwestern menu includes special children's selections.

# PARAMOUNT RANCH

This dusty Old West "ghost" town in the Santa Monica Mountains looks like every gunfightin', shoot-'em-up, corral town you've ever seen on TV or in the movies. And there's good reason for that. A fixture here since Paramount built the place in 1927, the town has been featured in numerous big- and small-screen hits, including *The Flintstones, Cousin Skeeter,* and, most recently, *Dr. Quinn, Medicine Woman.* Cinematic purists will be happy to know that such old-time classics as *The Adventures of Marco Polo* and *The Cisco Kid* were filmed here as well.

Your children will probably be more fascinated by the way the town looks, however, than by what's been shot—or should we say filmed?—here. Resembling a true relic abandoned after the days of stagecoaches and covered wagons, the town is dressed up or down depending on what, if anything, is being filmed. If you're lucky, you might actually catch a production in progress.

**KEEP IN MIND** If you're interested in learning about the movie and television history that was made here, come on the first or third Saturday of the month, when rangers lead one-hour "Set & Screen" tours. The free tours depart at 9:30. Another way to soak up the atmosphere is during one of the ranch's lively festivals, such as the Topanga Banjo Fiddle Contest (May), the Calabasas Pumpkin Fest (October), and a Chili Cookoff (October). The ranch can get extremely hot in the late summer; it's a good idea to bring water and a snack (though water fountains can be found on site).

Cornell Rd., Agoura

 Free

 Daily 8–sunset

805/370-2301

 All ages, hike 6 and up

Though it's all movie illusion, the Paramount Ranch nevertheless feels authentic, emitting that haunting, ethereal feel of a real-life ghost town. All the cliché establishments are here: feed and grain store, saloon, hotel, train depot, and livery—all that's missing are horses, and you might see those here, too. A picnic on the train platform really makes you feel as if you're in another era, and all those second-floor railings look like prime places for cowboys to come busting through at the climax of a good gunfight. Though the shops are all closed for business, the exteriors make for great photo ops and imaginative play.

Apart from the in-town scenery, the ranch has plenty of scenic hiking trails, including the ¾-mile Coyote Canyon and Medea Creek trails and the more difficult ½-mile Overlook trail. All are open to hikers and horseback riders, pardner.

**TRANSPORTATION** Getting to the ranch will require some driving, as it is in a somewhat remote area. Take the Ventura Freeway (U.S. 101) to the Kanan Road exit. Travel south on Kanan for ¾ mile, turn left on Cornell Road, and veer to the right. The entrance is 2½ miles down Cornell Road on the right.

**KID-FRIENDLY EATS** Though the town is indeed abandoned, there are plenty of picnic benches around (as well as rest rooms). **Applebee's** (3980 Thousand Oaks Blvd., Thousand Oaks, tel. 805/496–9444) serves the chain's usual selection of dependable burgers, sandwiches, and entrées. **Romano's Macaroni Grill** (4000 E. Thousand Oaks Blvd., Thousand Oaks, tel. 805/370–1133) features a large variety of pastas, as well as pizza, sandwiches, and a children's menu.

# PETERSEN AUTOMOTIVE MUSEUM

Southern Californians are known for their fascination with anything automobile-related. Extravagant cars are so common here that the average Beverly Hills parking lot (valet, of course) looks more like a luxury sports-car dealership. If you want to get close to some classics without setting off a cacophony of car alarms, come to this shrine to that most prized of southern California accessories: the automobile.

With three floors of exhibits, the Petersen does its job well, offering a glimpse into California's road-faring past and a chance to ogle a large collection of prized cars, from vintage to cutting-edge. The first floor's turn-of-the-century Streetscape invites you to walk through a colorful time in automotive history and actually board an old-time trolley. Multilingual computers furnish additional information. Upstairs, rotating galleries showcase famous Hollywood vehicles—the yellow New York City cab from *Seinfeld* and Herbie the Love Bug, to name two—as well as more contemporary hot rods and motorcycles.

## HEY, KIDS!
See if your family can work together to motor a model car's "combustion engine." As in a real car, the pistons are activated by spark plugs (in this case, human ones). If you all time your footwork, you can turn the crankshaft and make the car move.

**KEEP IN MIND** Annual membership at the Petersen is a particular bargain because it includes unlimited admission to the Page Museum, the Natural History Museum, and the William S. Hart Museum (*see* Natural History Museum for details). You'll also get an opportunity to come to the museum's annual Open House—available only to members—when the facility throws open the "vault" (actually the basement storage facility) and exhibits some of the vintage autos that are not part of its display collection.

 6060 Wilshire Blvd., at Fairfax Ave.

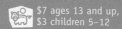 323/930–2277

 $7 ages 13 and up, $3 children 5–12

 T–Su 10–6

3 and up

For kids, the real fun stuff is most definitely in the museum's third-floor Discovery Center. Opened in 1997, this collection of interactive gizmos lets them unravel the science of driving and even experiment a little behind the wheel. Among activities are a giant dashboard complete with working gauges and a "truck" with age-appropriate activities. Kids love the turn-of-the-century Model T and accompanying period clothes as well as the California Highway Patrol motorcycle that emits sound effects when you take a seat. The most popular by far (as evidenced by the BE FAIR, DON'T FORGET TO SHARE sign posted on it) is the Driver's Education Simulator. Pint-size drivers strap in and "drive" a virtual course that appears on screen, choosing from three levels of difficulty. You know you're in trouble when the computerized voice chides, "Speeding in a school zone is a big ticket," so set a good example for your children and check your road rage at the door. You'll all have a truckload of fun.

**KID-FRIENDLY EATS** The food at fun **Ed Debevic's** (134 La Cienega Blvd., Beverly Hills, tel. 310/659–1952) is almost beside the point. The crazily clad wait staff at this '50s-style café serves burgers and other satisfying fare, and jumps up and dances about once every hour. In the ultratrendy Beverly Center, the **Hard Rock Cafe** (8600 Beverly Blvd., Beverly Hills, tel. 310/276–7605) serves burgers, fries, salads, and all the rock 'n' roll memorabilia you can stomach.

# PRACTICALLY PERFECT TEA

Put on the lacy frock, don the chapeau, and raise your pinky: Dressing up was made for this. Such is the fancy of taking high tea with Mary—Mary Poppins, that is—the magical nanny made famous in literature and film. Though it's not exactly the Ritz, the second-floor parlor of the Disney Pacific Hotel makes for a pleasant and child-friendly affair. Dainty music plays while mothers, grandmothers, and daughters (we're not trying to be sexist here; it's just that the overwhelming sentiment seems to be that it's just not a "guy" thing) sip tea and dish crumpets from perches in elegant settees.

Visitors to this Victorian delight will first have to make that all-important beverage decision: coffee, tea, . . . or chocolate milk? Light snacks, all served on delicate china, include scones with a variety of dainty jams, finger sandwiches (cucumber, turkey and mango, and chicken salad, among them), and pastries. Little ones can enjoy a plateful of delicacies created especially for them. Kid-specific fare includes the indispensable PB&J as well as Mickey-shaped waffles.

**KEEP IN MIND** This pleasant little affair manages to be sweet without being cloying. If you aren't in the mood for the cutesy Disney version, however, there are more so-phisticated (albeit more expensive) tea-totaling options available throughout the fashion-able streets of Beverly Hills. (Actually, adults can request champagne at some, for an extra fee.) A few to try: the **Peninsula** (tel. 310/551–2888), the **Regent Beverly Wilshire** (tel. 310/275–5200), and the **Four Seasons** (tel. 310/273–2222).

Disneyland Pacific Hotel, 1717 West St.,
off I-5, Anaheim

714/956-6755

$21.95 ages 13 and up,
$13.50 children 12 and under

Sa 10, 12:30, and 3; Su 12:30 and 3;
M, W, and F 12:30

3 and up

And of course there's plenty of tea—English breakfast, hot cinnamon spice, black cherry, and peach fruit—some in decaf versions so everyone can try them.

While you nibble, Mary appears, singing songs and sharing some of the wisdom that has made her so popular on the nanny circuit. The best part comes after the song and dance numbers, when Mary goes table to table, chatting about her days with the Banks family and dispensing advice about proper etiquette. (Don't even think about putting your elbows on the table or saying "super-califragilisticexpialidocious" with your mouth full!) Act Two brings Mary back center stage for a song-and-soft-shoe finale. Afterwards, everyone can try on some of Ms. Poppins's elaborate garb (the big hats and boas are favorites) and pose for pictures.

**KID-FRIENDLY EATS** If the tea's light fare doesn't fill you up, try the **PCH Grill,** on the hotel's first floor. Here grown-ups eat classy fare, while kids make their own pizza. At **Tiffy's** (1060 W. Katella Ave., tel. 714/635–1801), you can fill up on comfort food or Italian or Mexican favorites, but leave room for some homemade ice cream (try the chocolate peanut butter). Entrées start at about $6; most kids' meals run $4.

# QUEEN MARY

S wing music from the 1930s plays as you cross the gangway onto this grande dame of ocean liners. With much of its original splendor intact, the *Queen Mary* is a step back in time, an exercise in living history. The best part is that you get all the inherent adventure of a cruise ship at sea without ever leaving port—and hence, never getting seasick.

Thanks to richly paneled hallways and original fixtures, it's easy to imagine the *Queen Mary* in her heyday. Look for pictures of the luminaries who sailed on her, including Elizabeth Taylor, Bing Crosby, and Alfred Hitchcock, in one of the ship's photo galleries.

But much of the fun here—as on any cruise ship—is exploring the many areas on board, and there are plenty, from multiple decks and restaurants to numerous shops sprinkled around. Unlike a working cruise ship, the *Queen Mary* has an engine room that's open for inspection, and you can actually mosey right up to the Wheel House without a personal invitation

## HEY, KIDS!
About those ghosts, some visitors say they've spied a beautiful woman in a white gown dancing in the shadows of the Queen Salon or flashy damsels in 1930s-style swimming togs. Others claim to have heard splashing from the ship's long-drained pool. What do you think you'll see?

**KEEP IN MIND** First-Class discounted passes include admission to both the *Queen Mary* and the *Scorpion* (*see below*). Since you needn't see them on the same day, why not sandwich your visits around an overnight stay on the *Queen Mary*? Rooms run $75–$400 per night (less costly rooms are on the small side). Many original appointments remain, and modern luxuries have been added. Every Tuesday, the Queen Salon hosts big-band dancing (free with admission) 12–2. Before going home, stop at the adjacent Queen Mary Seaport, an old-fashioned village with shops, food, and an arcade.

from the captain. Your child won't be able to steer the ship, though, as it's permanently docked, after all.

Historic exhibits here include crew quarters, preserved just as they were during the ship's sailing days. More interesting, however, are the passenger-oriented exhibits, including the barber shop, the gym, the chapel, and even a playground, all hauntingly preserved as if previous passengers were about to return. (In fact, numerous on-board ghost sightings indicate they just might.) There are also several rooms depicting the ship during its Grey Ghost days—the period during World War II when she was painted gray and used as a military transport. (Hitler reportedly offered a reward worth $250,000 to the crew of any sub that could bring the *Queen Mary* down.) It's a blessing to all of us that no one succeeded.

**KID-FRIENDLY EATS** Downstairs, the **Grand Salon** (formerly the ship's first-class dining area) hosts a divine weekly Sunday brunch 10–2. The **Sundeck Deli** provides counter-service sandwiches, hot dogs, salads, and snacks—not to mention some tasty-looking pastries. Out in the Queen Mary Seaport, you'll find the type of food you'd expect at the **Queen's Barbecue** and **Market Place Pizza.** (Also *see* eateries in the *Scorpion*.)

# RAGING WATERS

I f you're looking to get wet, this is the place. Since its opening in 1983, this sprawling park has cooled off about 8 million visitors, and it's been labeled by a trade organization as one of the five most popular water parks in the nation. And no wonder. In an area known for some pretty toasty temperatures, Raging Waters is indeed a great place to keep cool.

About 30 minutes east of the city, the colorful park has appealing landscaping that manages to sidestep that sterile, cement feel often characteristic of such establishments. But the big draw here is the size (50 acres) and the scope (50 attractions). There's something for everybody, and new attractions are added to the park annually.

Daredevils will want to head straight for the Dropout, one of those fall-off-the-side-of-the-earth contraptions that you'll find either exhilarating or terrifying. Cross your arms and legs and plunge down a seven-story drop in roughly four seconds. (Note: one-piece bathing suits are recommended.) For anyone keeping score, there are also a couple of record-setters here,

**HEY, KIDS!** Raging Waters' newest addition, the Wedge, mimics the extreme-sport experience of skateboarding (think of a half pipe on a street course), with a few moments where you actually go uphill. The best part is that you get to pick how you ride—forwards, backwards, or sideways. The extreme effect is so inspiring, one couple used it to launch their nuptials; they said "I do" at the top and then sped down to the bottom (honest).

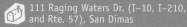  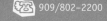

such as High EXtreme, at 100 feet tall (200 steps up), the tallest head-first slide in the world. Other thrill attractions have characteristically ominous names, such as the Dark Hole, the Vortex, and the Bermuda Triangle.

Although even the smallest children can turn inexplicably fearless here, less-adventurous tots (and their grown-ups) will find plenty that includes them in the fun. The Kids Kingdom actually looks like a typical neighborhood playground, only with sprinklers, sprays, and mini tube slides. Families can also have lots of fun climbing and sliding at both the Volcano FantaSea, a slide and splash area inside a "volcanic mountain," and Splash Island Adventure, a five-story aquatic climbing sculpture.

**KID-FRIENDLY EATS** There are plenty of places to eat inside the park, including the **Pizza Place** and **Burgers 'n' Fries.** Outside in the cute little town of San Dimas, you'll find a number of comfortable restaurants, including **Applebee's** (674 W. Arrow Hwy., tel. 909/394–7600), which serves burgers, sandwiches, salads, and ribs.

**KEEP IN MIND** Raging Waters alters its hours to keep up with daylight; in midsummer, you'll be able to keep sliding well into the evening. And there are other ways to get the most for your money, so be sure to ask about any promotions. If you plan to come often, check out the reasonably priced 20-visit and annual passes.

# RIPLEY'S BELIEVE IT OR NOT! MUSEUM

I f you've ever wondered about eight-legged pigs and two-headed cows, Ripley's is for you. Astounding, unbelievable, and more than occasionally a little gross, Ripley's is also a ton of fun, amounting to the museum equivalent of a car wreck in that you just can't keep from looking.

Across the street from the Movieland Wax Museum (*see above*)— Ripley's companion museum, operated by the same company—Ripley's "Odditorium" contains such unusual wonders of modern civilization as Sam Simpson (a wax figure of him, anyway); known as Three Ball Charlie, he could hold a tennis ball, golf ball, and billiard ball in his mouth all at the same time. There's also a wax likeness of Liu Ch'ung, who was born with two pupils in each eye—another of those gross entries. Lest you think the museum is simply a tribute to weirdness (although there is a lot of that), it also has some fascinating tidbits about nature that fall under the category of "education." Your children can learn that grasshoppers have five eyes and that caterpillars possess an unexpectedly large muscle mass. The museum itself even has some

## HEY, KIDS!

Want to become a conductor—not of a symphony or even of a train, but of electricity? Touch a knob and the metal post on the Human Conductor exhibit, and the radio begins to play. The gadget works because you complete an electrical circuit.

**KEEP IN MIND** Combining visits to Ripley's and Movieland will get you a discount at the ticket office, but it's best done over a couple of days. You'll have to use half of your pass the day you buy it, but the companion ticket is good indefinitely. Both museums are open year-round, with crowds most likely during school breaks. Even so, peak-season visits can be surprisingly uncrowded and make for a perfect air-conditioned diversion.

7850 Beach Blvd., Buena Park

714/522-7045

$8.95 ages 12 and up,
$5.25 children 4–11

M–F 11–5, Sa–Su 10–6

All ages

rather interesting lore attached to it. Modern legend has it that women who have touched the African Fertility Totems, which circulate among the nation's Ripley museums, have soon after become pregnant (parents, take this as a warning).

Visionary Mr. Ripley, a wax figure of whom stands guard in the front lobby, makes for pretty entertaining reading, too. The nondrinking, nonsmoking, eccentric bachelor cartoonist, who died in 1949, was an oddity in and of himself.

While many consider Movieland and Ripley's to be complementary experiences, if you're doing both in one day, you may want to leave more time for the latter. Even young children seem to find the outrageous displays here curious, leading to unusually long attention spans—perhaps the biggest "Believe It or Not" of all!

**KID-FRIENDLY EATS** You'll find a little bit of everything—Tex-Mex food, hot dogs, ribs, sandwiches, and salad—at **Spoons California Grill** (7801 Beach Blvd., tel. 714/523–1460). Kids eat free with a paying adult every Tuesday night. For entertainment, try **Medieval Times Dinner & Tournament** (7662 Beach Blvd., tel. 714/521–4740) or **Wild Bill's** (7600 Beach Blvd., tel. 714/522– 6414), both of which have theme performances as well as plentiful food. Also *see* Movieland Wax Museum.

# SANTA ANA ZOO AT PRENTICE PARK

Many people like this pleasing zoo in the heart of Orange County because it's small and easily walkable. Goldilocks would like it because it's "just right"—not too big, not too small, and with just enough surprises to entertain all members of the family without exhausting them. The zoo's 8-acre size will particularly appeal to you if you're pushing a stroller or leading an unsteady toddler. The zoo has also taken little ones' wandering attention spans to heart, providing a good-size playground at the entrance and a good rock-climbing spot at the zoo's center.

But the animals are most definitely the real stars here. Ostriches, monkeys, kangaroos, and mountain lions are among the zoo's 250 animals on display. Most are visible in their habitats, but there are a couple of roosters that amuse and surprise visitors by walking around (and crowing) freely. The newest and most striking of the attractions is the Colors of the Amazon exhibit. Large and well-landscaped, this walk-through aviary features streams, ponds, and a rain forest. Take heed when entering: The rain forest is authentic right down to the showers.

**HEY, KIDS!** Check out the Sounds Heard 'Round the World chart in the children's zoo. It translates animal sounds into different languages. So you can learn, for example, that "oink" translates into Japanese as "ink, ink bubu." Do you think animals really sound different in different countries? If an animal moves, does it have to become bilingual to communicate with its new furry friends? Nah, we're just pulling your paw.

If you happen to enter during one of the manmade downpours (12:30 and 3:30, but only on the hottest summer days), you can count on getting very wet.

Your kids can get an extra kick out of some exhibits by using a Zoo Key, available at the park entrance. Keys inserted into designated boxes by some exhibits will yield a bit of information about that animal as well as an accompanying song.

In addition to the main exhibits, there's a good-size children's zoo, where you'll find the usual suspects—sheep, pigs, goats, and even some snakes (the latter, thankfully, in glass cases). Though the zoo's wide paths are mostly paved, the children's zoo has dirt roads—ostensibly to go along with the Old McDonald's Farm feel of the red barnyard structures—making it, oddly, the hardest place to push a stroller.

### KEEP IN MIND

Recent additions to the zoo include the Zoofari Express, one of those scale-model trains that will cost you $1 to ride. The train runs Friday, Saturday, and Sunday from 11 to 3. A bit of trivia: If the train looks familiar, it probably is; the entire set (engine to caboose) was relocated from the now-defunct Santa's Village in the San Bernardino Mountains.

### KID-FRIENDLY EATS

The zoo's on-site **snack bar** serves burgers, hot dogs, sandwiches, and, not surprisingly, snacks. Drive a little way up I-5 to the Main Place shopping center (2800 N. Main St., tel. 714/547–7000), where you can choose from a food court and sit-down restaurants, together offering a taste of everything. Some favorite chain restaurants are **California Pizza Kitchen** (tel. 714/479–0604) and **Ruby's** (tel. 714/836–7829); the former serves tasty pizzas and pastas, whereas the latter is known for burgers, sandwiches, and salads.

# SATWIWA

Children expecting movie-variety Indians at this Native American cultural education center are in for a surprise. The focus at Satwiwa is on Native American culture, 1990s style. "People expect to see us in 500-year-old feathers," explains a Satwiwa park ranger. "Here, they get a rare chance to come face-to-face with contemporary Indian people in what may be the only place they get to do that."

Located in the heart of the Santa Monica Mountains, the Satwiwa center sits on a lovely expanse of land with its roots in Chumash history (the name Satwiwa—which means "the bluffs"—was that of a nearby village long ago). Though you can hike the trails here anytime and visit the cultural center the whole weekend, the best day to come is Sunday, when you can visit with one of the Native American hosts. In addition to enthusiastically discussing their culture and answering questions on the subject, these volunteers (representing all the Pan American people) demonstrate such crafts as beading, basket weaving, and rug making, occasionally inviting children to participate. One day, for example, an affable

**KID-FRIENDLY EATS** The **Black Angus Steak House** (139 W. Thousand Oaks Blvd., Thousand Oaks, tel. 805/497–0757) also serves chicken and seafood, while **Outback Steak House** (137 E. Thousand Oaks Blvd., Thousand Oaks, tel. 805/381–1590) has Australian flair.

**KEEP IN MIND** If you'd like to visit on a Sunday in order to see one of the Native American hosts, ask about the schedule of Charlie Cooke, a Chumash chief and well-loved Native American guide, who draws huge crowds for his four annual walks. Adventurous hikers may want to take advantage of the 70 miles of hiking trails at the adjoining Point Mugu State Park. Trails along here tend to be steep and rugged—more appropriate for older, more adventurous kids. Check with park rangers before setting out.

Lynn Rd. and Via Goleta, Newbury Park

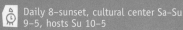 Daily 8–sunset, cultural center Sa–Su 9–5, hosts Su 10–5

 Free

 5 and up

805/370-2301

Creek Seminole woman named Jane told legends of her culture and demonstrated the art of making ceremonial Ribbon Shirts, the garb commonly worn during powwows. The center occasionally features Native American dancers and storytellers, and powwows are planned for the future. If you're not lucky enough to happen upon one of these majestic pageants in person, you can watch a video. Inside, exhibits and books depict past and present Native American life.

Satwiwa's open terrain makes for some scenic hiking, and easy-to-manage trails traverse the area. The best hike for kids is the Satwiwa Loop Trail, a 2-mile round-trip that takes you past a windmill and along an overlook of Satwiwa.

**TRANSPORTATION** Take U.S. 101 to Lynn Road south; travel 5¼ miles, and turn left on Via Goleta, the park's main entrance road. (Note: Via Goleta is easy to miss; if you pass the Dos Vientos housing development on your right, you've gone too far.) The large main parking lot is the last one, about ¾ mile down the Via Goleta. (If you park in an earlier lot, you'll have a long walk.) The Satwiwa site is about ¼ mile from the lot.

# SCORPION

Kids seem to be universally fascinated by anything that floats, so imagine what your children will think of a vessel that travels underwater! The *Scorpion,* an actual Soviet submarine moored next to the *Queen Mary (see above;* discounted combination tickets available), provides a look at this incredible method of aquatic travel. Though a far cry from Captain Nemo, this black Cold War craft (commissioned in 1972) nevertheless inspires more than a few exclamations of "cool!"

You start with a bit of submarine history via an orientation film at the sub's entrance. While you do learn some details about the size (300 feet long), speed, and capacity of the vehicle, don't expect a serious scientific study. This film is so utterly hokey that it's actually entertaining.

Still, it's the submarine itself that's the focal point. The entire interior is open, and you can pass through all seven compartments, examining the mechanics and weaponry (there were once 16 nuclear-tipped torpedoes on board; today one disarmed torpedo remains) as well as

KEEP IN MIND The entrance sign warns that the tour will be like an obstacle course. It's no joke. Ladders are steep but easily maneuverable if you're wearing good shoes; heels are a mistake, as are dresses! A busy day makes the sub feel crowded, which may bother you if you're claustrophobic. Though motion is generally negligible, the vessel is partially under water and does occasionally sway, so beware if you're prone to seasickness. Finally, be careful if you're tall. Even someone as small as 5′ 2″ will occasionally have to duck so as "not to bump head," as the Russian-accented voice warns.

1126 Queens Hwy., southern end of I-710, Long Beach

 562/435-3511

$10 ages 12 and up, $9 children 4–11

 Daily 10–6

5 and up

where the crew ate, slept, worked, and kept secret documents. A chirpy Russian-accented voice prompts you from one compartment to the next, dispensing little factoids, such as that the vessel has only two bathrooms and one shower (for 78 men!), that its boardroom doubled as its operating theater, and that sailors didn't wash dirty sheets—they just threw them away. (Is it any wonder the Soviet Union no longer exists?) Though the sub technically works, the instruments have been deactivated, so children can push, pull, and turn wheels without doing any damage. Of course, don't bother trying to figure out what the gadgets are for; notations are in Russian.

Most striking are the accommodations: A vast luxury liner it isn't. In fact, despite its exterior size, the inside is remarkably cramped. Although there's generally room for tourists to move around—with only a few spots where you'll have to suck in your gut to pass someone—it's hard to imagine a crew of 78 holed up in here for months at a time.

**HEY, KIDS!** Be sure to peer into the periscope—"the eyes of the sub." It really works. Once you've seen what you can see outside, see what you can hear inside by using the phone. First find the extension number of the compartment you're in. Then have a family member go to a different compartment and crank the phone to call you. It's not an overseas call; it's an underseas call.

**KID-FRIENDLY EATS** Eating spots at the adjacent Queen Mary Seaport include the **Londontowne Deli and Bakery;** get takeout and grab one of the tables spread around the seaport. **Shoreline Village** (401–435 Shoreline Dr.), a quaint retail hamlet that's also good for biking, has **Tugboat Pete's** (tel. 562/436–4919), for burgers or barbecue sandwiches on the go, and the scenic **Parker's Lighthouse** (435 Shoreline Dr., tel. 562/432–6500). Also see the Queen Mary.

# SIX FLAGS HURRICANE HARBOR

A sprawling water mecca alongside its sister park, Magic Mountain, Hurricane Harbor is the place to go to cool off on those blistering-hot summer days. Though not quite as artfully done as some other water-park incarnations—lots of uncamouflaged cement gives the place a less than tropical feel—the ambience is inconsequential when temperatures reach up into the triple digits. And the slides and rivers are indeed a lot of fun. As one cool-and-comfortable dad observed, "If you've got a pent-up 5-year-old and it's 106° out, this is the only place to be!"

The fact that 5-year-olds can have as much fun here as their older siblings is one of the best features of this young park. Divided into theme areas, Hurricane Harbor strives to entertain the whole family with a varied selection of 22 daring slides, lazy rivers, and water attractions.

Little ones can get cooled off at Castaway Cove, where mini slides and waterfalls cater to the under-54" crowd. There's more water play at Shipwreck Shores, where you and your

**KEEP IN MIND** Water shoes and dry clothes are suggested. There are lockers ($3 per day, rented at the entrance) and showers on site. Tubes, required for certain rides, can be rented for the day ($4 singles, $6 doubles). Finally, ask about discounted combo admission with Magic Mountain.

**HEY, KIDS!** Challenge your sibling (or parent) to take on Bamboo Racer. The six-lane water race is partially affected by weight (alas, the heaviest usually goes fastest), but littler ones can increase their odds: Don't lie flat on your "water toboggan," the mat you ride on. Instead, lie on your back but keep your head up; pull back; and lean into those curves. You might just win.

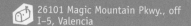 26101 Magic Mountain Pkwy., off
I-5, Valencia

 661/255-4111

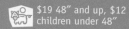 $19 48" and up, $12
children under 48"

  Mid-May and mid-Sept, Sa-Su 10-6; Memorial Day-Labor Day, M-F 10-6, Sa-Su 10-8

All ages

children can splash around in a number of areas, including an oversize skull. Thrill slides include open and closed varieties, from the 75-foot-tall Black Snake Summit to the 130-foot-long Reptile Ride to the 65-foot-high Venom Drop. (Can Fang Falls, Cobra Creek, and Python Plummet be far behind?) Prospective thrill seekers can get their first look at Venom Drop from the parking lot, where the near-vertical slide seems to tower over the parked cars. On your way in, you can watch prospective plungers climbing the stairs up and up and up, not to mention the dramatic slide down.

Hurricane Harbor thrills are not as extreme as those next door at Magic Mountain, but since each park's rides are essentially adjacent to the other's, it's hard to tell where all the squeals and screeches are coming from.

## KID-FRIENDLY EATS

Several **snack shops** dot the park. **Red Eye's Kitchen,** the only on-property restaurant, serves rotisserie chicken, burgers, dogs, and salads. Outside park gates and down the street, **Hamburger Hamlet** (27430 The Old Road, tel. 661/253– 0888) has basic chain-restaurant fare. (Get your hand stamped when you leave the park for same-day reentry.) If you're in a bring-your-own mood, there's a picnic area in the parking lot. You'll have to keep the eats in your car, however, as coolers aren't allowed.

Kids who like their rides scary—terrifying, actually—will find unparalleled excitement here. If Disneyland has introduced your children to theme parks, this is where they earn their stripes, surviving a mind-boggling collection of loops, drops, and yes, even, bungee jumps (or a reasonable approximation) on their way to one of the ultimate thrill experiences.

The park has 10 so-called monster coasters, including Flashback, which gives the sensation of a free fall, and Revolution, the world's first looping coaster. Though riders may think they're having all the fun, there's much entertainment in the spectator arena, watching the wide-eyed faces of loved ones as they soar up a 41-story incline at 100 mph (that would be Superman the Escape) and loop around (and around!) on the world's longest, fastest stand-up coaster (Riddler's Revenge). But even bystanders are bound to get a little skittish at the sight of comrades soaring from a cord down the 150-foot drop on Dive Devil. ("Watching her do it is thrill enough for me," quipped the boyfriend of one diver.) Dive Devil is so popular that you'll have to make reservations upon arrival at the park and pay an extra fee that varies by whether you fly solo, double, or triple.

**HEY, KIDS!** Your parents may put the kibosh on Dive Devil (even if the 48" minimum height doesn't), but you can still feel like you're defying gravity on Superman and Freefall, both of which feature significant drops that create a momentary feeling of weightlessness. Hold onto your stomachs!

 26101 Magic Mountain Pkwy., off I–5, Valencia

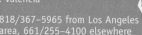 818/367–5965 from Los Angeles area, 661/255–4100 elsewhere

$39 48" and up, $18 under 48"; Dive Devil additional $15–$25

Late Mar–June, Su–Th 10–8, F–Sa 10–10; July–Labor Day, Su–Th 10–10, F–Sa 10 AM–12 AM; early Sept–mid-Mar, Sa–Su 10–6

 2 and up

Not all the rides here are so extreme; the less adventurous can find happiness at the Grand Carousel or the Log Jammer flume ride. Of course there are plenty of kiddie rides, particularly at the newly remodeled Bugs Bunny World, whose 11 rides include the pint-size Canyon Blaster roller coaster. There are no height requirements here; you just have to fit snugly into the harnesses, and a new rule allows parents to ride along.

But Magic Mountain visitors pay for thrills (not to mention the park's liability insurance), so if you're toting only smaller children, you're probably best off at a tamer, less expensive establishment (*see* Adventure City). Even if the prospect of abject terror doesn't detour your young thrill seekers, the height requirements (most grown-up rides post a minimum height of 48") probably will.

**KEEP IN MIND** Like many other amusement parks, Magic Mountain is most crowded in the summer. Families who visit after Labor Day may get the place virtually to themselves, as many people are unaware that it, unlike its next-door neighbor and sister, Six Flags Hurricane Harbor (*see* above), is a year-round operation. During the summer, ask about discounted Magic Mountain/Hurricane Harbor combo admission, and look for occasional discounts available through fast-food chains and on soft-drink containers.

# SOLSTICE CANYON

Of all the colorful hikes in the Santa Monica Mountains, this one is my family's very favorite. Shady and lush with the ocean breeze providing cool relief on even the hottest southern California days, the Old Sostomo Road route in Solstice Canyon is scenic hiking at its best, a place where wide pathways and flat terrain make it possible for even the youngest children to put on their sneaks and enjoy. A wonderful getaway from the L.A. hubbub, it might as easily be called Solace Canyon.

The old road takes you along a maze of gurgling creeks. Though you may be tempted to stray into them, rangers caution against it; besides, even on the hottest days, the water's c-c-c-cold. Listen along the way for the rustling sounds of wildlife, including tiny lizards that regularly scurry across your path. There are plenty of tadpoles around, too, as well as scads of colorful butterflies.

**KEEP IN MIND** Though the terrain is largely flat, only about ⅔ of the route is paved. After that, strollers become tough to push. Your safest bet is to don the old backpack carrier. If you do, you'll want to take the right (stream-side) fork near the end of the trail. Call the Visitor Center (tel. 805/370–2301) to learn about other trails.

**TRANSPORTATION** Take the Pacific Coast Highway to Corral Canyon Road north. Travel ¼ mile to the park entrance, on the left. It's important to note that the park entrance is marked by a rather inconspicuous white gate. If you make a hard right turn and find yourself winding through the Santa Monica Mountains, you've definitely gone too far.

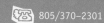

For many people, the trip's highlight is Tropical Terrace, the remains of a mansion burned to the ground in the 1980s. Though its 1950s construction date makes the house less than an antique, there's nevertheless something otherworldly and ethereal about it. While much of it is gone, stone structures such as patios, fireplaces, and a few rooms remain—all overgrown with tropical greenery, hence the name—making for some neat stomping grounds to explore.

If you're speeding along, you can probably travel the entire 2.1-mile Sostomo Road trip in about an hour. But this is definitely a "stop and smell the roses" tour—or at least a "stop and watch the lizards" tour. Your kids will no doubt want to linger around waterfalls and rocky areas, whereas the Tropical Terrace makes a perfectly serene spot for a family picnic. Other Solstice Canyon trails, such as the Sostomo Loop and the Rising Sun trails, are a good deal more challenging, taking you right through the mountains and occasionally requiring you to push aside brush to get through. They are best for experienced hiking families with preteens and teens.

**KID-FRIENDLY EATS** An obvious choice is to pack a picnic. However, if you're tired of making sandwiches, you can dine overlooking the beach at **Malibu Fish and Seafood** (25653 Pacific Coast Hwy., tel. 310/456–3430), known among locals for its really fresh and reasonably priced seafood, from fish-and-chips to swordfish. Supposedly, nothing is more than two hours old. **Gladstone's 4 Fish** (17300 Pacific Coast Hwy., Pacific Palisades, tel. 310/454–3474) is also popular for seafood and features some landlubber's selections, too.

# SPEEDZONE

Young adolescents pining for their licenses can see how their driving prowess stacks up against Mom's and Dad's at this miniature raceway built for amateurs. A veritable speed-demon fantasy land, the 12-acre park features five tracks—the Top Eliminator, Grand Prix, Slick Trax, Turbo Track, and SideWinder—on which you can careen and compete in scaled-down versions of the race cars you see on TV.

Experiences range from tame to extreme. The most exhilarating, Top Eliminator, is truly of the "Peel Your Eyelids off Your Forehead" variety the brochures purport it to be. Drivers in 300-hp dragsters get to control acceleration and shifting—no steering necessary, as Top Eliminator cars run on a metal rail—and race three other drivers down a 140-yard stretch. Cars go from 0 to 70 in three seconds. The short but memorable experience is gloriously authentic: Christmas Tree lights start you out of the gate, and a force equivalent to three g's throws you back in your seat. Braking, thankfully, is done by computer at the finish line.

**KID-FRIENDLY EATS** The **Terrace Bar** offers full-service meals alongside the arcade. Outside the park, you can continue the car theme at **Frisco's Car Hop Diner** (18065 Gale Ave., tel. 626/913–3663). It features roller-skating waitresses, classic-car booths, and diner favorites.

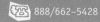
 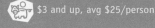

Other SpeedZone tracks focus more on skill than sheer adrenaline. In Slick Trax, for example, drivers need to master the art of cornering and braking through turns in order to maneuver the ultraslippery road surface without skidding. All tracks have electronic scoreboards to display times, and you and your children can take home printouts of your accomplishments.

Since professional race drivers consulted on the design, SpeedZone feels like the real thing or, as the brochures again boast, "The closest thing to professional racing offered to the public." For safety, cars have been designed low and wide to avoid tipping. In the event of a problem, all vehicles can be instantly shut down from a central control station.

Some tracks charge by the minute and others by the lap. There is also an extensive arcade as well as two miniature golf courses in case your need for speed abates.

**HEY, KIDS!** Among SpeedZone's arcade games are virtual skateboards and Jet Skis, which you can either play by yourself or link up to a friend's game for a race. In fact, arcade game races can accommodate as many as eight competitors. Still other arcade games furnish tickets that you can redeem for prizes. Just think of all the ways you can spend your parents' money.

**KEEP IN MIND** Anyone at least 5' tall with a valid driver's license is automatically authorized on all tracks. Those 13 and up who meet height requirements but don't have a license are limited to the Turbo Track and Top Eliminator; to experience the other tracks, they have to pass a preliminary test, offered through the so-called SpeedZone Racing School on select Saturdays. Instruction is free, but the necessary track time costs about $22. Children under 13 who are at least 42" tall can ride with an adult driver on Turbo Track. After 9 nightly, SpeedZone is open only to those 18 and older.

# TELEVISION TAPINGS

Lots of Los Angeles attractions take you behind the scenes to reveal how shows are produced, but only one activity enables you to actually see a production take shape: the studio-audience experience. Virtually every live-studio-audience show is up for grabs, including *Frasier* and other popular fare. Though viewers may feel privileged to garner a seat, the producer/audience relationship is a symbiotic one. Tourists can watch their favorite stars, while producers get bodies to supply those all-important audience reactions.

Audience members find a festive, party atmosphere thanks largely to comedians who act as congenial masters of ceremonies between takes. You also get a firsthand look at outtakes you just might see later on one of those myriad bloopers shows. The downside can be the time required and tedium that sets in if take after take of the same scene is required. In fact, don't be surprised if a ½-hour sitcom takes several hours to complete.

**KEEP IN MIND** Paramount isn't the only show in town. Audiences Unlimited (tel. 818/753–3470) handles many productions, but for the most popular, you'll have to request tickets at least a few weeks ahead. For some, you'll have to write. Contact NBC (3000 W. Alameda Ave., Burbank 91523, tel. 818/840–3537) for the *Tonight Show with Jay Leno*, or try arriving at the studio at 8 AM, when a limited number of same-day passes (maximum two per person) are distributed. For all shows, get to the studio at least 90 minutes before taping time. Like airlines, productions overbook to ensure plenty of guffawers, and you can be bumped.

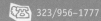 Paramount Pictures, 5555 Melrose Ave.

 323/956–1777

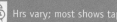 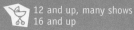 Hrs vary; most shows tape M–F evening

Free

12 and up, many shows
16 and up

If you're open to seeing any taping—not necessarily a specific program—you can often find same-day tickets (on weekdays, when nearly all shows tape) by calling Paramount. The most easily accessible passes, however, are likely to be for new shows and pilots for which producers need to build audiences. That could mean watching something wonderful or something dreadful—after all, even *The Magic Hour* had an audience . . . once. At Paramount, even the hot tickets don't require months of advance planning. Reservations for Paramount programs are taken a maximum of five days out—even for popular shows—giving everyone a fair shake.

When making your all-important booking, be sure to ask about age requirements, as they vary from show to show. Most shows' producers like their audiences on the older side (roughly 16 and up), not just for the production's content, but also for the shenanigans that ensue between takes. Elementary schoolers, however, aren't totally left out; some shows (particularly those associated with kids' networks) welcome guests as young as 8.

**KID-FRIENDLY EATS** If you're attending an evening taping, you'll want to grab a bite first. You'll find Korean barbecue at **Woo Lae Oak** (623 S. Western Ave., tel. 213/384–2244), where individual hibachi grills enable you to cook your own dinner at your table (unless, of course, you do enough cooking at home). If your taping takes you to the Burbank area, try the **Hard Rock Café** (1000 Universal Center Dr., Universal City, tel. 818/622–7625), where atmosphere and people-watching overshadow the adequate salads, burgers, and sandwiches.

# TRAVEL TOWN MUSEUM

I f your kids are like most, they've probably imagined themselves in the cab of an old-time locomotive. To make their dreams come true, bring them to this storybook land of actual antique engines. It's guaranteed to toot the whistle of any pint-size engineer.

This low-key and unassuming little marvel in a region known for big-bang attractions is nevertheless a gold mine of imaginative playthings. It's a retirement home for long-since-derailed vintage locomotives and passenger cars, where kids can climb aboard, daydream, and explore. Consisting of several dozen old stalwarts (40 at last count), the collection includes everything from an 1880 Southern Pacific locomotive to a 1910 Western Pacific caboose, not to mention turn-of-the-century Los Angeles railway trolleys and an 1880 horse-drawn railway car. The 1864 Stockton Terminal & Eastern No. 1 is a kid favorite because of its red and black design that seems to have come out of a story. The number and configuration of trains changes, so you'll have to look around for what you want to see.

**HEY, KIDS!** Look for the scale-model train layout (weekends only). Running through city and countryside, the train setting is filled with working parts, such as crossings and a turntable, and clever details, such as tiny clothes hanging between buildings. How many details can you find?

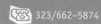
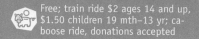

Other novelties include wagons and automobiles significant in Los Angeles history and an exhibit building with antique fire engines and related equipment.

You can mill about the entire yard, weaving in and out of these iron maidens that stand idle on antique tracks. Some of the collection can be climbed aboard; others are there just to look at. Although the antique behemoths will no doubt inspire fantasies of great train robbers making dramatic escapes across the train tops, your kids will have to imagine it all from the ground, as no one is allowed to scale the outside or roofs of the trains. The equipment is stationary except for the charming ride-on train that chugs around the park's perimeter—directed by a classically dressed conductor, of course—and a restored circa-1941 diesel engine that hooks up to two cabooses each month (usually the first full weekend) and takes passengers on a few-minute trip along the length of the museum. All aboard!

**KID-FRIENDLY EATS** For on-the-spot eats, there's the **Dining Car** (tel. 323/662–9840), a window-service snack shack whose menu includes hot dogs, chicken, pizza, and snacks. **California Pizza Kitchen** (101 N. Brand Blvd., Glendale, tel. 818/507–1558) offers the franchise's tasty pizzas and salads within about a 10-minute drive.

**KEEP IN MIND** Though you can climb inside some vehicles, you'll spend much time milling about outdoors, so you'll want to pick a day when heat or rain isn't an overwhelming factor. If you're looking for the ideal birthday party, ask about a special package that includes celebrating aboard one of the park's two World War I–vintage passenger cars. Other good news: Lead paint has already been re-moved from these vintage vehicles' accessible areas.

# UNIVERSAL STUDIOS HOLLYWOOD

I f you can't actually be in the movies, the next best thing is to "ride" them—precisely the premise of this theme park built around a working film studio. A conglomeration of flight simulators, special-effects encounters, thrill rides, and soundstages, Universal is an extreme version of Disneyland—a place where fantasy becomes a very vivid reality.

Attractions incorporate themes from popular movies, some worth riding for the scenery, such as the "bike ride" through E.T.'s homeland (E.T. Adventure), others for thrills. If you're a flight-simulator fan, you won't want to miss *Back to the Future*—The Ride, an unparalleled jostle through time in Doc Brown's trademark DeLorean. Special-effects enthusiasts will be impressed by *Backdraft,* in which you actually feel flames, and *WaterWorld*—A Live Sea War Spectacular.

Many of the park's trademark elements (Jaws, King Kong, Earthquake—The Big One) can be found on Universal's back-lot tram tour. Though the gimmicks make for a good time, having to see them combined into one package can make the tour feel excruciatingly long—

## HEY, KIDS!

Don't miss the opportunity to "slime" Mom and Dad. Nickelodeon Live is a feast of parent-humbling fun. If you get them on stage, you can cheer as they get slimed, slapped with a pie, or made into a human hamburger. Want to up the odds of getting picked? Choose an aisle seat.

**KEEP IN MIND** The shows at Universal are for all ages, but there isn't much in the ride department for the under-7 set. In the shoe department, nix the sandals here. The upper-lot/lower-lot layout makes for a lot of walking. Before leaving Universal City, make sure to get an eyeful of the Universal Studios CityWalk, which contains restaurant/clubs, unusual shops, and some pretty interesting people-watching.

 100 Universal City Plaza., off U.S.
101, Universal City

 818/508-9600

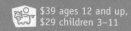 $39 ages 12 and up,
$29 children 3–11

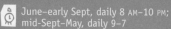 June–early Sept, daily 8 AM–10 PM;
mid-Sept–May, daily 9–7

 6 and up

particularly with young children. However, since some of the effects here are pretty intense, you might want to rethink taking little ones anyway. *Jurassic Park*—The Ride, a flume trip down an 85-foot drop, is a hoot if you like this sort of thing. But be warned that you're best off doing this one late in the day, as you won't get wet, but rather completely soaked. (Disposable raincoats—a particularly good idea in winter—are sold at the ride's entrance.) The newest addition is *Terminator 2:* 3D, a live-action, 3-D film/special-effects gig that definitely packs a punch.

Universal also has a couple of shows worth seeing, most notably Nickelodeon Live, which re-creates the "slimy" game show atmosphere made famous by that kids' network. Some of the park's un-dead (Dracula, Frankenstein, and the Wolfman, for example,) rock and roll at Beetlejuice's Rockin' Graveyard Review. And any little kids you've brought are sure to love the Animal Actors Stage, with furry (and too-cute) performers aplenty.

**KID-FRIENDLY EATS** Universal has food carts, restaurants, and cafeterias. For retro, try **Mel's Diner,** a '50s-style hop. In addition to ribs, chicken, and burgers, **Marvel Mania** (1000 Universal Center Dr., tel. 818/762–7835), just outside park gates, is loaded with wacky gimmicks, such as vibrating seats.

# UPPER NEWPORT BAY ECOLOGICAL RESERVE

I f ever there was an antidote to the Los Angeles hustle and bustle, this ecological reserve is it. A rare find amid the beach scenes and expensive homes of most southern California coastal communities, Upper Newport Bay, an estuary an hour south of the city, can really make you and your family feel you've gotten away from it all.

The most popular way to enjoy the area is by boat—specifically canoes and kayaks. Most Saturday mornings, the reserve's volunteer naturalists lead visitors on scenic canoe paddles around the area. Alternatively, you can book a Sunday kayak tour through Resort Watersports at the Newport Dunes Resort (tel. 949/729–1150); these trips cost more but start later in the morning and can accommodate children as young as 2. Either way, tours run about two hours, with roughly 2–3 miles' worth of paddling.

The bay is home to large, colorful, and, in many cases, rare birds, which you can spy while enjoying this serene wetland. (Surprisingly, spring, fall, and winter scenery is best.) Birds

HEY, KIDS! Look for the dramatic fishing style of ospreys, which swoop down to the water and grab fish in their talons. They typically nest in eucalyptus trees but are hard to spot. Their nests, however, can often easily be seen in trees and on buoys in channels. To spot baby birds, look in late spring.

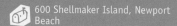 600 Shellmaker Island, Newport Beach

 949/640-6746

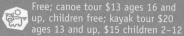 Free; canoe tour $13 ages 16 and up, children free; kayak tour $20 ages 13 and up, $15 children 2–12

 Daily 8–sunset, canoe tour Sa 8:30, kayak tour Su 10

 Canoe tour 7 and up, kayak tour 2 and up

to look for include members of the heron family, such as great blue herons and snowy egrets, as well as the occasional pelican. Many of these local residents are large—about 3' tall with wing spans up to 6'—making them particularly captivating to young children. Once in a great while, you might even spy a sea lion.

If you'd prefer to go it alone, the adjacent Newport Dunes Resort rents kayaks hourly as well; you'll just have to stay off the islands and in the boat. (The resort [tel. 949/729–3863] also has a lagoon to swim in and watercraft and bicycles for rent.) Devout landlubbers can enjoy the scenery via the ecological reserve's free guided nature walks, on the first and third Saturdays of every month, or by taking a self-guided walk any day.

Both reserve and resort offer other children's activities, including summer evening camp fires.

**KID-FRIENDLY EATS** The Newport Dunes Resort's **Back Bay Café** (1131 Back Bay Dr., tel. 949/729–1144) serves hamburgers, sandwiches, and a children's menu. Not far from the reserve, **Joe's Crab Shack** (2607 W. Pacific Coast Hwy., tel. 949/650–1818) serves fresh seafood bay-side; kids like the pizza, chicken fingers, and hot dogs.

**KEEP IN MIND** On request, the canoe tour fee will cover California Wildlife Campaign membership, entitling you to a year's unlimited canoe trips and half-price kayak trips. Rangers suggest reserving three weeks ahead for canoe tours. Though Resort Watersports is mostly open weekends only, you can arrange for boat rental at any time by calling during operating hours. Contact Amigos de Bolsa Chica (Warner Ave. and Pacific Coast Hwy., Huntington Beach, tel. 714/840–1575) about walking tours of the Bolsa Chica Ecological Reserve.

# VANS SKATEPARK

**5**

Snag your board, Ollie up to the handrail, grab Indy, land, and ride 50-50 down the rail. (In English, for you parents, that's roughly translated as riding straight down a handrail.) This place is heaven on wheels.

Vans, known worldwide as a leading skateboard equipment manufacturer, has provided a whiz-bang haven for local extreme sporters. Open since 1998, the mammoth, 46,000-square-foot mecca stood briefly as the world's largest—that is until Vans opened a few bigger, even fancier ones in other parts of the country. Nevertheless, enthusiasts and pros (both boarders and in-line skaters) continue to scope the place out in droves. On any given day, your kids may be Ollie-ing around with the likes of Omar Hassan, Steve Caballero, or Jen O'Brien—and though you may not know who they are, your kids probably will.

In addition to banks and ledges, boarders will find a bit of nostalgia in the form of the Combi Pool, an exact replica of the world-famous Upland Pipeline Skatepark course that

## HEY, KIDS!

Look for details about the Vans Amateur World Championships of Skateboarding, an elite event held at the park annually in November. Admission is free. Though the park is emptiest during school hours, don't even think about cutting class to get in; Vans does a check on all school-age kids.

## KEEP IN MIND
All boarders/skaters are required to wear helmets, knee pads, and elbow pads. Wrist guards are optional. Safety equipment can be rented on-site; other equipment is BYOB (bring your own boards and blades). If you're a serious skater, consider a $50 annual membership, which cuts your per-session price; savings will start to add up if you're going once a month or more.

20 City Blvd. W, I-5 and Rte. 22, Orange

 714/769–3800

 $11–$14/session (varies with time of yr and hrs)

 July–Labor Day, daily 8 AM–11 PM; early Sept–June, 10 AM–11 PM

4 and up

closed in the 1980s. The Combi is the most technical of Vans's three pools, notable for being in-ground, a superior (and more expensive) alternative to the above-ground pools found at most public parks. To boot, there's an 80-foot-wide vertical ramp and 18,000-square-foot street course. If you're up for learning a new trick or two, try the free lessons that are included in the two-hour session fee (no reservation required). The place even has a designated peewee area for budding roller enthusiasts of all ages (for practical purposes, we're talking from about age 4); bring your own skates if you plan on accompanying your kids, as no pedestrians are allowed on the floor.

Vicarious thrill seekers (and the simply faint of heart) can look out over the action (for free) from the 6,000-square-foot mezzanine. From there, you can feel safe in the knowledge that the skate areas are patrolled by a competent, first-aid-trained staff.

**KID-FRIENDLY EATS** The Block at Orange, the mall that is home to Vans, houses a typically vast number of fast-food and snack haunts ranging from **Jody Maroni's Sausage Kingdom** to **Starbucks Café**. If you're in more of a sit-down mood, try the **Wolfgang Puck Grand Cafe** (tel. 714/634–9653) or **Johnny Rockets** (tel. 714/769–4500).

# VENICE BEACH

I f you're looking for a beach scene as opposed to just a beach, nothing beats the spectacle that is Venice Beach.

This diverse sand-side habitat is practically a monument to funkiness, with sunbathing coming in a distant second to the featured attraction: people-watching. This is a character mecca, a perpetual parade of pedestrians, bikers, and rollerbladers all marching to the off-beat. Street performers, too, are the rage. On any given day, a stroll along Venice's paved walkway can get you front-row seats before many varied demonstrations of skill, including—but certainly not limited to—impressionists, hip-hop dancers, and chain-saw jugglers. You can marvel from the sand or pull up a chair at any of the beach-side cafés that provide the perfect venue from which to watch the show unfold.

Venice is also home to that famed outdoor palace of physical fitness, Muscle Beach, where rippling Arnold Schwarzenegger wannabes (legend has it that the Terminator was discovered

**KID-FRIENDLY EATS** The **Sidewalk Cafe** (1401 Ocean Front Walk, tel. 310/399–5547) has standard favorites right on the beach. The **Rose Café** (220 Rose Ave., tel. 310/399–0711) offers indoor or outdoor seating and everything from swordfish to pizza.

Western end of Venice Blvd., Venice

 Free

  Recommended 8–sunset

310/396–7016 Venice
Chamber of Commerce

12 and up

here) pump themselves up inside a chained-off area while a field of onlookers gawk from the other side. Real people get their exercise up and down the paved walkway that runs for a few miles along the beach. You can bring your own rollerblades or bikes or rent them at one of the nearby shops. If you do opt to do this, however, be prepared to have plenty of company as the Venice walkway is one of the busiest thoroughfares around.

As for retail, there's good news and bad news. The good news is that there are plenty of funky shops peddling sunglasses, beach paraphernalia, tarot-card readings, and more. The bad news, however, is that you may have to steer your teenager away from those proprietors hawking body piercings and tattoos. Hey, we're talking Venice here!

**HEY, KIDS!** Venice was created in 1905 by Abbot Kinney, a tobacco magnate from New Jersey. Local myth has it that Kinney wanted to re-create his favorite Italian city. In reality, creating canals was just the easiest way to drain the marshland. Colorful residents arrived early on. One was Jake Cox, who, in 1914, used to attract folks to his indoor pool by dressing in a fuzzy suit and setting himself on fire.

**KEEP IN MIND** Venice, as a family undertaking, is definitely recommended as a daytime activity. Prepare yourself for some unseemliness (it's better territory for sexologists, than for young children) and some conversation afterwards. On the other hand, a little family communication isn't so bad, and the biking, skating, and even canoeing are great; for the latter, contact Venice Canoes (tel. 310/396–1344). To learn the whole cool truth about the city, take a tour with the Venice Historical Society (tel. 310/967–5170). Tours (holidays only) cost $15.

# WARNER BROS. STUDIOS TOUR

One of the lures of Hollywood is that you never know whom you're going to run into, and many people are drawn to this studio tour for just that reason. However, though star encounters certainly happen here, they are the exception, not the rule. You'll probably have to content yourself with a look at movie-studio magic—pretty thrilling in and of itself—and the knowledge that a celebrity—Noah Wyle, perhaps—could be somewhere in the vicinity.

Those familiar with the theme-park variety of back-lot tour (such as at Universal Studios Hollywood) may be pleasantly surprised here. However, on that note, this educational and historical tour is definitely for more mature audiences. This is the real (or perhaps reel) thing—more intimate and less schtick-laden. You tour in intimate groups via golf carts, rolling through the lot while knowledgeable guides spin tales of studio legend and lore. Every tour is different, with what you see dependent upon what's filming and what areas are open that day. In fact, some people take the tour several times. A typical day might include a trip through

**KID-FRIENDLY EATS** Universal Studios CityWalk features the **Wolfgang Puck Café** (1000 Universal Dr., Universal City, tel. 818/985–9653), serving the famous chef's brand of California cuisine. People in the "biz" are rumored to like **Dalt's** (3500 W. Olive Ave., tel. 818/953–7750), a hospitable American grill.

**KEEP IN MIND** The roughly 2¼-hour tours require walking (occasionally on loose surfaces) so wear good shoes. Though tours operate year-round, encountering work in progress is less likely during hiatus periods around Christmas and in late spring/early summer. Reservations are required, but last-minute visitors can occasionally be accommodated. Also try the Paramount Studios Tour (5555 Melrose Ave., tel. 323/956–1777) or the shorter (70 minutes) tour given by NBC (3000 W. Alameda Ave., tel. 818/840–3537).

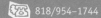 Hollywood Way and Olive Ave., Gate 4, Burbank

 $30

 818/954–1744

June–Aug, M–F 9–4 every ½ hr; Sept–May, M–F 9–3 every hr

12 and up

the wardrobe department, followed by some photo ops in front of the trolley diner featured on *ER*. (Only still cameras are allowed, and photography may be limited.) A fun stop—if it's not in use for a production—is the studio's Old West town set, where you can look for the blind school from *Little House on the Prairie* as well as the saloon familiar from such Westerns as *Maverick*.

True movie aficionados will no doubt be in heaven here, but even non-movie buffs are bound to be delighted. Yes, thousands take the tour each year, but you will nevertheless feel like you're getting VIP treatment. The excursion, in fact, is actually named the VIP Tour, because it was originally created to entertain visiting dignitaries during the studio's early years.

*HEY, KIDS!* Complete the "insider" experience by perusing the racks at It's a Wrap! Productions (3315 W. Magnolia Blvd., tel. 818/567–7366), where you can purchase outfits last worn in your favorite TV shows and films. Half the fun is owning a piece of Hollywood; the other is getting great bargains, such as a Banana Republic shirt (perhaps worn in *Beverly Hills, 90210*) for $5. You won't find the stars' clothing (those are pricier items categorized as "collectibles"), but you'll get a conversation piece.

# WILDLIFE WAYSTATION

U nder ordinary circumstances, coming face to face with a lion would be cause for panic. At the Wildlife Waystation, it's an occasion for awe. Close encounters of the wildlife kind are the hallmark of this unique facility in the Angeles National Forest. Unlike a zoo, where hundreds of feet typically separate humans and beasts, animals encountered here—about 1,100–1,200 at any one time, including lions, tigers, coyotes, primates, and bears—are only a few feet away, separated by their enclosures. That means you'll "get close enough to hear them purr," as one recent guest put it, and can appreciate the full size of, say, a Bengal tiger. And when all 60 lions roar, as they occasionally do, "you can hear it all throughout the canyon," says founder Martine Colette.

Such proximity can be accomplished only at a rare place like the Waystation. While zoo residents need a human comfort zone because of their daily showings, animals here receive guests only one or two days a month and by appointment only (in other words, reservations are required). The infrequent company diminishes the animals' stress level and allows them to feel comfortable up close and personal.

**HEY, KIDS!** More than 5,000 animals come through the Waystation annually. Wild animals (North American residents like raccoons and deer) are often returned to the wild. Exotic animals from around the world are either transferred to appropriate homes or stay here. Iguanas are always plentiful, mostly because well-meaning folks get them as pets and don't know what to do when they grow. Before adopting any pet, make sure you know the facts so you can care for it for its lifetime.

14831 Little Tujunga Canyon Rd., 5 mi off I–210, Angeles National Forest

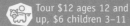 Tour $12 ages 12 and up, $6 children 3–11

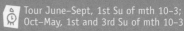 Tour June–Sept, 1st Su of mth 10–3; Oct–May, 1st and 3rd Su of mth 10–3

818/899-5201

 5 and up

Far from just an animal showcase, Colette's creation is a sanctuary, a place where animals come when they have nowhere else to go. Some have been abandoned, others became homeless after the closing of a circus or zoo, while still others have been rescued from inappropriate keepers who have mistreated them.

A private institution (Colette bought the 160-acre canyon spread after her traditional suburban home could no longer accommodate her "finds," such as a cougar), the Waystation is licensed by all animal authorities at the local, state, and federal levels, meaning all enclosures meet or exceed specified guidelines. Though education is paramount here, one of the other great perks is the walk through the serenely rural surroundings—only ½ hour from Los Angeles but nevertheless another part of the world.

**KID-FRIENDLY EATS** Wildlife Waystation's canyon location makes it remote from many restaurants. About 10 minutes away, in Sunland, you'll find numerous fast-food joints as well as a **Coco's** (10521 Sunland Blvd., tel. 818/353–5677), a diner-style eatery with sandwiches, burgers, and the like. About 15 minutes away, in Pasadena, there's much more to choose from.

**KEEP IN MIND** Children younger than 5 can be accommodated, but you'll probably need to carry them, at least part of the time. This is definitely not a stroller-friendly park—terrain is rugged and unpaved. Sunday tours run roughly 70 minutes. During the summer, the Waystation offers several Saturday evening tours in darkness. These strolls occur at a time when nocturnal animals—normally lounging during the day—can be seen and, more importantly, heard. The price for the evening walks includes an on-site dinner but is only for visitors 16 and up.

# WILD RIVERS

With some of the world's most sought-after attractions nearby, you might think that home-grown Wild Rivers just wouldn't stack up. Nothing could be further from the truth. A compact water park with a bit of neighborhood appeal, it still manages to offer about 40 attractions in total: some to cool you off, others to warm you up, and a good supply of slides that can literally thrill the swimsuit right off of you.

Prospective sliders can pretty much guess the nature of the ride by its moniker. If it's named something like the Ledge, the Edge, or the Abyss, it's a sure bet that you'll be flinging yourself down something winding, fast, and scary. Wipeout hurls you down a slide ahead of 1,000 gallons of water, while Chaos, predictably, is similarly disorienting. Bombay Blasters shoots you out like a cannonball, so hold onto your trunks. You can also float on a lazy river or choose your brand of wave-pool surf from either the gentle current of Monsoon Lagoon or the cranked-up waves of Hurricane Harbor (the latter for expert swimmers only).

**HEY, KIDS!** The Patriot, a four-person in-line flume ride, stands seven-stories tall, the only one like it in southern California. Wonder why it's called the Patriot? The red, white, and blue flume seems to resemble a Patriot missile, and you'll feel like you're rocketing as you career forwards and even backwards for a time. Tip: If you're on the small side, stock your boat with some bigger folks (a couple of dads wouldn't hurt). The heavier you are, the faster you'll go.

8770 Irvine Center Dr., off I–405, Irvine

949/768–9453

$23 ages 10 and up, $18 children 3–9

Mid-May–mid-June and early–late Sept, Sa–Su 11–4; late June–Labor Day, daily 10–8

2 and up

Thrills here are mercifully not (if you'll pardon the expression) over the edge. There's plenty to get wet and wild on, but preteens—even the daring ones—seem to like Wild Rivers' slides for being scary, but not too scary. Little kids like their chance to slide like the big kids (the kiddie sections have miniature versions of some of the big-people attractions), whereas parents generally laud Wild Rivers for being small enough so they can keep an eye on their youngsters at all times.

In fact, size seems to be the big bonus here. When compared to other water parks—nearby Raging Waters, for example, is more than twice as big—Wild Rivers is intimate. You won't feel as though you're trekking miles to get from one ride to another, and you can go home feeling like you've actually done it all. Don't think, however, that that means your kids won't want to come back. They will—repeatedly.

**KID-FRIENDLY EATS** Wild Rivers has all the basics— sandwiches, fries, and snacks—at **Colonel Hawkin's.** It also contains the **Congo Cafe,** for pizza, as well as the **Sweet Shoppe,** an ice-cream place. After an exhausting day of getting wet, warm your belly with rotisserie chicken and mashed potatoes at **Boston Market** (13125 Jamboree Rd., tel. 714/505–3600).

**KEEP IN MIND** The Hurricane Harbor wave pool is for expert swimmers 54" and taller only. You'll need a boogie board to surf, and you can rent one at the central Rental Shack for $4 per day. Lockers and inner tubes are also available for rent. Ask about discounted "Dry" passes for visitors arriving as spectators only and "Car Load" discounts, offered late June–Labor Day, Mondays 4–8. The cost is $40 per carload, up to eight; after that, it's an additional $5 per person. Additionally, individual passes go down to $12 (ages 3 and up) after 4 PM.

games

# THE CLASSICS

**"I'M THINKING OF AN ANIMAL..."** With older kids you can play 20 Questions: Have your leader think of an animal, vegetable, or mineral (or, alternatively, a person, place, or thing) and let everybody else try to guess what it is. The correct guesser takes over as leader. If no one figures out the secret within 20 questions, the first person goes again. With younger children, limit the guessing to animals and don't put a ceiling on how many questions can be asked. With rivalrous siblings, just take turns being leader. Make the game's theme things you expect to see at your day's destination.

**"I SEE SOMETHING YOU DON'T SEE AND IT IS BLUE."** Stuck for a way to get your youngsters to settle down in a museum? Sit them down on a bench in the middle of a room and play this vintage favorite. The leader gives just one clue—the color—and everybody guesses away.

# FUN WITH THE ALPHABET

**"I'M GOING TO THE GROCERY..."** The first player begins, "I'm going to the grocery and I'm going to buy... " and finishes the sentence with the name of an object, found in grocery stores, that begins with the letter "A." The second player repeats what the first player has said, and adds the name of another item that starts with "B." The third player repeats everything that has been said so far and adds something that begins with "C" and so on through the alphabet. Anyone who skips or mis-remembers an item is out (or decide up front that you'll give hints to all who need 'em). You can modify the theme depending on where you're going that day, as "I'm going to X and I'm going to see..."

**"I'M GOING TO ASIA ON AN ANT TO ACT UP."** Working their way through the alphabet, players concoct silly sentences stating where they're going, how they're traveling, and what they'll do.

**FAMILY ARK** Noah had his ark—here's your chance to build your own. It's easy: Just start naming animals and work your way through the alphabet, from antelope to zebra.

**WHAT I SEE, FROM A TO Z** In this game, kids look for objects in alphabetical order—first something whose name begins with "A", next an item whose name begins with "B," and so on. If you're in the car, have children do their spotting through their own window. Whoever gets to Z first wins. Or have each child play to beat his own time. Try this one as you make your way through zoos and museums, too.

# JUMP-START A CONVERSATION

**WHAT IF...?** Riding in the car and waiting in a restaurant are great times to get to know your youngsters better. Begin with imaginative questions to prime the pump.

- If you were the tallest man on earth, what would your life be like? The shortest?
- If you had a magic carpet, where would you go? Why? What would you do there?
- If your parents gave you three wishes, what would they be?
- If you were elected president, what changes would you make?
- What animal would you like to be and what would your life be like?
- What's a friend? Who are your best friends? What do you like to do together?
- Describe a day in your life 10 years from now.

**DRUTHERS** How do your kids really feel about things? Just ask. "Would you rather eat worms or hamburgers? Hamburgers or candy?" Choose serious and silly topics—and have fun!

**FAKER, FAKER** Reveal three facts about yourself. The catch: One of the facts is a fake. Have your kids ferret out the fiction. Take turns being the faker. Fakers who stump everyone win.

# KEEP A STRAIGHT FACE

**"HA!"** Work your way around the car. First person says "Ha." Second person says "Ha, ha." Third person says "Ha" three times. And so on. Just try to keep a straight face. Or substitute "Here, kitty, kitty, kitty!"

**WIGGLE & GIGGLE** Give your kids a chance to stick out their tongues at you. Start by making a face, then have the next person imitate you and add a gesture of his own—snapping fingers, winking, clapping, sneezing, or the like. The next person mimics the first two and adds a third gesture, and so on.

**JUNIOR OPERA** During a designated period of time, have your kids sing everything they want to say.

**IGPAY ATINLAY** Proclaim the next 30 minutes Pig Latin time, and everybody has to talk in this fun code. To speak it, move the first consonant of every word to the end of the word and add "ay." "Pig" becomes "igpay," and "Latin" becomes "atinlay." To words that being with a vowel, just add "ay" as a suffix.

**BUILD A STORY** "Once upon a time there lived..." Finish the sentence and ask the rest of your family, one at a time, to add another sentence or two. Bring a tape recorder along to record the narrative—and you can enjoy your creation again and again.

**NOT THE GOOFY GAME** Have one child name a category. (Some ideas: first names, last names, animals, countries, friends, feelings, foods, hot or cold things, clothing.) Then take turns naming things that fall into that category. You're out if you name something that doesn't belong in the category—or if you can't think of another item to name. When only one person remains, start again. Choose categories depending on where you're going or where you've been—historic topics if you've seen a historic sight, animal topics before or after the zoo, upside-down things if you've been to the circus, and so on. Make the game harder by choosing category items in A-B-C order.

**COLOR OF THE DAY** Choose a color at the beginning of your outing and have your kids be on the lookout for things that are that color, calling out what they've seen when they spot it. If you want to keep score, keep a running list or use a pen to mark points on your kids' hands for every item they spot.

**CLICK** If Cam Jansen, the heroine of a popular series of early-reader books, says "Click" as she looks at something, she can remember every detail of what she sees, like a camera (that's how she got her nickname). Say "Click!" Then give each one of your kids a full minute to study a page of a magazine. After everyone has had a turn, go around the car naming items from the page. Players who can't name an item or who make a mistake are out.

**THE QUIET GAME** Need a good giggle—or a moment of calm to figure out your route? The driver sets a time limit and everybody must be silent. The last person to make a sound wins.

# THEMATIC INDEX

# ACKNOWLEDGMENTS

Writing this book took the help (and patience!) of some extraordinary people. My thanks go to all the Los Angeles area PR people—particularly Carol Martinez and Stacy Litz at the Los Angeles Convention and Visitors Bureau and Elaine Cali and Jennifer Gonzalez at the Anaheim Orange County Visitor & Convention Bureau—who kept answering my phone calls no matter how many hundreds of times I called. To all my LA friends who stuck with me as I dragged them through yet another Los Angeles attraction—I couldn't have done it without you. More thanks to my oh-so-wonderful editor, Andrea Lehman, who made the book more literate and the process more fun. To my daughters, Alexis and Melissa, who put up with way too many hours of mommy writing—I love you. And finally, to my incredible husband, Steve—without your patience, sense of humor, and late-night omelets, this book would never have happened.

—Lisa Oppenheimer

the end